WARM UPS
TO MAXIMISE PERFORMANCE

50 WARM UP PRACTICES | YOUTH TO PRO | TRAINING WEEK | FOOTBALL PERIODIZATION

Written by

ADAM OWEN PhD

UEFA Pro Coaching Licence

Published by

WARM UPS
TO MAXIMISE PERFORMANCE

50 WARM UP PRACTICES | YOUTH TO PRO | TRAINING WEEK | FOOTBALL PERIODIZATION

First published May 2024 by SoccerTutor.com
info@soccertutor.com | www.SoccerTutor.com

UK: 0208 1234 007 | **US:** (305) 767 4443 | **ROTW:** +44 208 1234 007
ISBN: 978-1-910491-68-3

Copyright: SoccerTutor.com Limited © 2024. All Rights Reserved.

All rights reserved. No part of this publication may be reproduced, stored in a retrieval system, or transmitted in any form or by any means, electronic, mechanical, photocopy, recording or otherwise, without prior written permission of the copyright owner. Nor can it be circulated in any form of binding or cover other than that in which it is published and without similar condition including this condition being imposed on a subsequent purchaser.

Written by Adam Owen

Edited by Alex Fitzgerald - SoccerTutor.com

Diagrams

Diagram designs by SoccerTutor.com. All the diagrams in this book have been created using SoccerTutor.com Tactics Manager Software available from www.SoccerTutor.com

Note: While every effort has been made to ensure the technical accuracy of the content of this book, neither the author nor publishers can accept any responsibility for any injury or loss sustained as a result of the use of this material.

CONTENTS

Dr. Adam Owen: Coach Profile 6
Dr. Adam Owen: Career of High Performance Expert 8
Dr. Adam Owen: Author 9
How this Book Fits into the "Football Periodization to Maximise Performance" Philosophy 10
Benefits of the "Football Periodization" to Maximise Performance Methodology 12
Diagram Key 13
Practice Format 13

The Training Week 14

Practice Design Considerations to Optimise Coaching Outcomes 15
Training Session Flow 16
Practical Coaching Model to Build the Training Week (Microcycle) 18
Periodization, Tapering Strategy and Maximising Performance 19
The Training Week: Professional Microcycle 20
Training Session Format for Professional Microcycle 21
The Training Week: Semi-Professional Microcycle 22
The Training Week: Youth Academy Microcycle 23
The Training Week: Grassroots (Youth) Microcycle 1 24
The Training Week: Grassroots (Youth) Microcycle 2 25
Analysis of a 6-Week Training Mesocycle and Positional Quantification in Elite European Football Players 26

Periodization of Warm Ups 27

Periodization of Warm Ups 28
General Warm Up Exercises Without the Ball Movement Examples 29
Considerations of the Microcycle (Training Week) 30
Progressive Intensity 31
Components of a Good Generalised and Preventive Warm Up 33

Resistance Warm Ups 34

Resistance Warm Up Practices 35
Effects Of Cutting Technique Modification on Change of Direction Performance 36
4 Days Until Match (MD +3/-4): Positional Principles and Resistance 37
Resistance Training Session: 4 Days Until Match (MD +3/-4) 38

4 Days Until Match (MD +3/-4): Resistance Warm Up Practices 39
Resistance 1. Agility, Coordination, and Balance Hurdle Exercises Warm Up Circuit 40
Resistance 2. Speed, Coordination, and Power Exercises 4-Station Warm Up Circuit. 41
Resistance 3. Coordination, Lateral Movement, and Quick Reactions Warm Up. 42
Resistance 4. The "Mirror" Technical Ball Control in Grids Warm Up 43
Resistance 5. The "Guantlet" Technical Ball Control and Moves to Beat Defenders Warm Up. 44
Resistance 6. Close Ball Control Skills Through Poles "Ronaldinho" Warm Up Circuit 45
Resistance 7. Lateral Speed of Movement and Ball Skills Dynamic Zig-Zag Warm Up Circuit. 46
Resistance 8. Coordination and Ball Control Skills Technical Warm Up Circuit. 47
Resistance 9. "Brazilian Fast Feet" Dribbling and Ball Control + Agility Warm Up Circuit 48
Resistance 10. Ball Control, Agility, Speed, and Coordination Technical Warm Up Circuit. 49
Resistance 11. "Resistance V" Warm Up with Various Technical Skills in Pairs 50
Resistance 12. One-Twos and "Switch" with Varied Movements Technical Warm Up 51
Resistance 13. Ball Control Skills "Nutmeg" Technical Warm Up in Pairs with Hurdle Gates 52
Resistance 14. One-Two, Move to Receive, and Dynamic Flexibility "In & Out" Pairs Warm Up. 53
Resistance 15. Varied Movements and Dynamic Flexibility Zig-Zag Warm Up Circuit 54
Resistance 16. Speed, Agility, and Coordination Technical "Give & Go" Warm Up Circuit. 55
Resistance 17. Speed, Agility, and Coordination Warm Up Circuit with Reactive "Tag Game". 56
Resistance 18. Speed, Agility, and Coordination Warm Up with Reactive "3v1 Possession" 57
Resistance 19. "Crossfire" Passing, Agility, and Speed 4-Corners Technical Warm Up. 58
Resistance 20. Attack vs Defence Warm Up with Passive Jockeying Movements 59
Resistance 21. Collective Team Pressing in Relation to Ball Position "Sacchi" Warm Up 60

Speed Endurance Warm Ups 61

Speed Endurance Warm Up Practices 62
3 Days Until Match (MD +4/-3): Collective Team Principle Training and Speed Endurance 63
Speed Endurance Training Session: 3 Days Until Match (MD +4/-3) 64
3 Days Until Match (MD +4/-3): Speed Endurance Warm Up Practices. 65
Hamstring Activity at Different Running Speeds 66
Speed Endurance 1. Dynamic Flexibility and Agility "Fast Feet" Warm Up Circuit. 67
Speed Endurance 2. Coordination and Fast Footwork "Crossover" Warm Up Circuit 68
Speed Endurance 3. Coordination, Agility, and Flexibility Varied Tempo Warm Up Circuit. 69
Speed Endurance 4. Coordination, Balance, and Flexibility Varied Tempo Warm Up Circuit 70
Speed Endurance 5. Dynamic Mobility, Agility, and Power Warm Up Circuit 71
Speed Endurance 6. Mobility, Coordination, and Sprinting Triangle Warm Up Circuit 72
Speed Endurance 7. Technical Stop, Start, Pass, and Running With the Ball Circuit Training. 73
Speed Endurance 8. Progressive Overload Speed and Agility Exercises Circuit Training. 74
Speed Endurance 9. Agility, Coordination, and Speed 4-Station "Pyramid" Circuit Training. 75

Reaction Speed Warm Ups ... 76

Reaction Speed Warm Up Practices ... 77
Key Information ... 78
2 Days Until Match (MD +5/-2): Unit Principle Training and Reaction Speed Development ... 79
Reaction Speed Training Session: 2 Days Until Match (MD +5/-2) ... 80
2 Days Until Match (MD +5/-2): Reaction Speed Warm Up Practices ... 81
Reaction Speed 1. Quick Footwork and Coordination Warm Up Exercises ... 82
Reaction Speed 2. "Rebounding" Changes of Direction and Agility Warm Up Circuit ... 83
Reaction Speed 3. Agility Exercises with Fast Feet and Changes of Direction Warm Up ... 84
Reaction Speed 4. Quick Footwork and Coordination Diamond Warm Up Circuit ... 85
Reaction Speed 5. Various 2-Footed Juggling Techniques Circle Warm Up ... 86
Reaction Speed 6. Technical Running With the Ball Quick Footwork at Speed Warm Up ... 87
Reaction Speed 7. Ball Control, Skills, and Quick Reactions to Commands Warm Up ... 88
Reaction Speed 8. "The Clock" Running Inside and Out Dynamic Warm Up ... 89
Reaction Speed 9. Zig-Zag Dribbling and Finishing at Speed Technical Warm Up ... 90
Reaction Speed 10. Coordination and Agility with One-Two Combination Warm Up ... 91
Reaction Speed 11. Agility Exercises + One-Two in Multi-Station Warm Up (1) ... 92
Reaction Speed 12. Agility Exercises + One-Two in Multi-Station Warm Up (2) ... 93
Reaction Speed 13. Lateral Coordination and Acceleration "Spin & Go" Warm Up ... 94
Reaction Speed 14. Speed, Coordination, and Awareness "Windows" Warm Up with One-Twos ... 95
Reaction Speed 15. Passing and Reactions for Speed Work in a 4-Grid Warm Up ... 96

Pre-Match Activation Warm Ups ... 97

Pre-Match Activation Warm Ups (Training the Day Before Match) ... 98
Effects of Warm Up, Post-Warm Up, and Re-Warm Up Strategies on Explosive Efforts in Team Sports ... 99
1 Day Until Match (MD +6/-1): Pre-Match Activation Training Day ... 100
Activation Training Session: 1 Day Until Match (MD +6/-1) ... 101
1 Day Until Match (MD +6/-1): Pre-Match Activation Warm Up Practices ... 102
Activation 1. Dynamic Stretching, Movements, and Sprints Double Circle "Juventus Warm Up" ... 103
Activation 2. Dynamic Stretching and Different Types of Movements Warm Up ... 104
Activation 3. Dynamic "Stop & Go" Speed Work with Changes of Direction Warm Up ... 105
Activation 4. Dynamic Movement, Agility, Fast Reactions, and Sprinting Warm Up ... 106
Activation 5. Mobility Movements and One-Twos in a Dynamic 2 Phase Warm Up Circuit ... 107
Activation 6. Quick Combinations and Support Play Passing Square Technical Warm Up ... 108

Advance Your Career: Become a Better Coach... ... 109
Adam Owen Performance Consultancy ... 110
References ... 111

Dr. Adam Owen: Coach Profile
UEFA Pro Coaching Licence

Dr. Adam Owen
PhD, MPhil, BSc HONS

@adamowen1980

www.aoperformance.co.uk

Academic Credentials (PhD):
- Doctor of Philosophy (PhD) in Sport Science and Coaching - Claude Bernard Lyon.1 University, Lyon, France

Coaching Credentials:
- UEFA Professional Coaching Licence - Football Association of Wales (FAW)
- FA Youth Trainers Award - England Football Association (FA)

Football Positions:
- High-Performance and Technical Advisor, KKS Lech Poznań, Poland
- Assistant Head Coach, Hibernian FC, Scotland
- High-Performance Director and Technical Advisor, Seattle Sounders FC, USA (MLS)
- High-Performance Director and Assistant Coach, Hebei China Fortune FC, China
- Head Coach, KS Lechia Gdańsk, Poland
- High-Performance Coach, Wales National Team
- Assistant Manager, FC Servette, Switzerland
- Assistant Manager, Sheffield United FC, England
- Head of Performance, Rangers FC, Scotland
- Head of Sport Science and Fitness, Sheffield Wednesday FC, England
- Head of Academy Performance and Technical Coach, Celtic FC, Scotland
- Academy Head Coach, Wrexham FC, Wales
- Player, Wrexham FC, Wales

Further Roles, Development and Associations:

- Football Consultant, Double Pass, Belgium
- Associate Researcher (Football Science and Performance) for Lyon.1 University, France
- UEFA Professional Licence and UEFA A Licence Coach Educator for the England Football Association (FA)
- UEFA Coach Educator for various other football federations
- Faculty Member and Lecturer for the International Soccer Science and Performance Federation (ISSPF) www.ISSPF.com
- Over 100+ papers published in international peer-reviewed journals including Journals of Sport Sciences, International Journal of Sports Medicine, Journal of Strength and Conditioning Research, International Sport Science and Coaching Journal, and many more...
- Football Consultant, SL Benfica, Portugal
- Director of Research (5 years), SL Benfica, Portugal
- Key Note Speaker at various international level conferences and congresses

Dr. Adam Owen:
Career of High Performance Expert

Dr. Adam Owen has forged a distinctive blend of hands-on coaching expertise, holding a **UEFA Pro Coaching Licence**, and an esteemed academic background in Football Science and Coaching. He earned his **PhD in Sport Science & Coaching** from Lyon.1 University in France and currently serves as an associate Professor at Glyndwr University in Wales. Additionally, he maintains an associate researcher role in France while actively contributing to the professional football arena.

Adam Owen's coaching journey encompasses diverse roles across elite youth and senior levels, including **UEFA Champions League** and **Europa League** competitions, European club football, and high-profile international football engagements. Notably, at the age of 26, Adam was integral to the management team of **Rangers FC** (Scotland), reaching the **UEFA Cup Final in 2008** and staying with the club for seven and a half years. His time there yielded invaluable experience in steering the team towards successful league and cup endeavours, alongside multiple UEFA Champions League campaigns.

In 2014, Adam embraced a new challenge by joining **FC Servette** in Switzerland, marking his venture into European club football while maintaining his role with the **Wales National Team (2009-2018)**. Adam contributed to Wales' journey to the **UEFA Euro 2016 Semi-Final** in France before assuming the position of **Head Coach at Lechia Gdansk** (Poland).

Subsequently, he ventured into the Chinese Superleague as a High-Performance Director, followed by a stint with MLS Champions **Seattle Sounders FC** (USA) as Technical Advisor and High-Performance Coaching Director. His achievements include clinching the **MLS Western Conference League Title** and reaching the **MLS Cup Final**.

Adam Owen's expertise extends beyond coaching, as he also serves as an **elite coach educator at UEFA Professional level for the England FA and other UEFA federations**. As Adam's career spans playing, coaching, coach education, high-performance expertise, management, and technical directorship, he has a **unique and wide scoping expertise in the football world**.

Adam has made substantial contributions to football literature, with over 100+ publications ranging from articles, book chapters, and books. He remains actively involved in advancing football-based research at the elite level and is a faculty member of the prestigious International Soccer Science and Performance Federation *(www.ISSPF.com)*, offering top-tier international online courses in football science and performance.

Drawing from his extensive domestic and international successes, Adam has developed a **research-based coaching methodology aimed at optimising individual and collective performance within elite professional football**.

Dr. Adam Owen: Author
Best Selling Football Conditioning Book Set

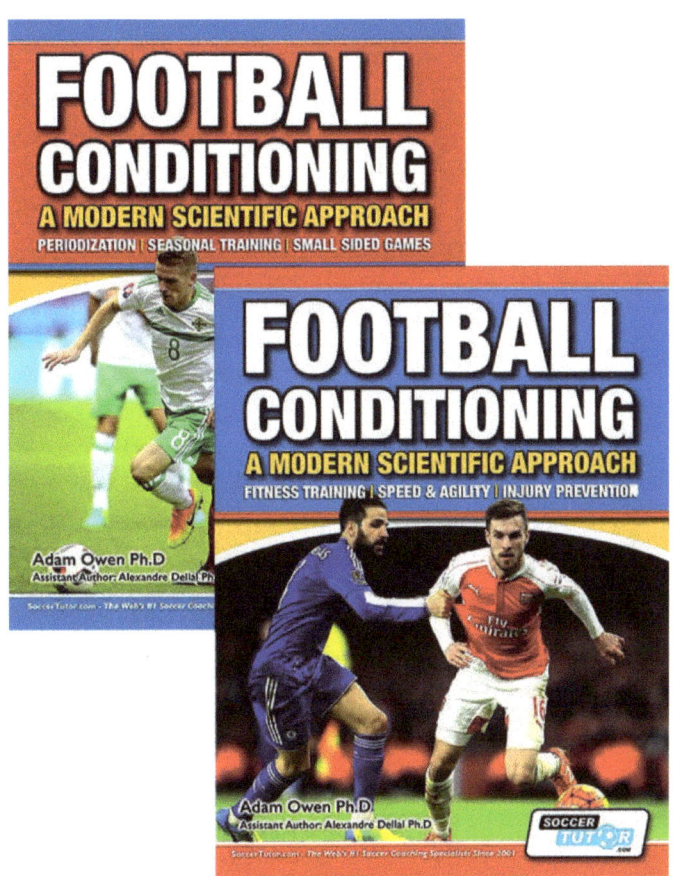

Available in English, German, and Spanish (Print & eBook)
Included: 130 Topics, 54 Practices, and 24 Exercises (U15-Pro)

 **FREE COACH VIEWER APP**

www.SoccerTutor.com

How this Book Fits into the "Football Periodization to Maximise Performance" Philosophy

- The **"Football Periodization to Maximise Performance"** book is a key resource.
- The **warm ups in this book form part of this philosophy** of a full training program, so it is **highly recommended to add this book to your library**.
- Written by world leading high performance expert, **Dr. Adam Owen**, and **available from SoccerTutor.com in full colour print and eBook**.
- Proven and successful football methodology to maximise the performance of your players and team.
- Adaptable training week model for Pro, Semi-pro, Academy and Youth levels with **102 Practices** included.
- Methodological approach and training plan to produce optimum conditioning, low injury rates, and high performance.
- Make sure your players are always prepared correctly and **perform at their maximum level on match day**.

Football Periodization to Maximise Performance Methodology:

- Enhance coaches' knowledge of high performance and coaching.
- Improve player performance and gain a competitive advantage.
- Maximise the training time and efficiency of the coaching process.
- Game model: Link the technical, tactical and physical details of the game.
- Maximising the use of specific training games and practices in the training week.
- Show the actual demands imposed on players in training and manage the training load to reduce injury risk.
- How to design training sessions.
- Planning the flow of the training week to maximise performance.
- Tapering strategy = players arrive in optimal condition for the match!

"Warm Ups" Within the Football Periodization to Maximise Performance Methodology:

The *Football Periodization to Maximize Performance Methodology* emphasises the vital role of tailored warm up routines in effective training sessions, regardless of players' skill levels.

Initiating each session with a carefully designed warm up, precisely attuned to match the specific physical and technical demands of the following practices in the session, forms the very foundation of effective practice organisation and player preparation. As you will find from the direct link between the two books *(this one and the Football Periodization book outlined on the previous page)*, which together form a comprehensive coaching curriculum and strategy, coaches are encouraged to incorporate warm up exercises that address the complete development of players, encompassing various aspects including physical conditioning, technical skills, and mental readiness.

Aligned with the principles outlined in the *"Football Periodization to Maximise Performance"* book, the process of designing practices seamlessly integrates with the overarching themes of the session, with a dedicated focus on **4 Primary Daily Physical Training Themes**:

1. Resistance Day

The focus is on **acceleration, deceleration, and directional changes**, incorporating practices of **high-intensity** and **small sided games** to nurture agility, cardiovascular progression, muscular strength, and resilience in players.

2. Speed Endurance Day

While the emphasis lies on reproducing **sustained bursts of high speed** (sprinting bouts), it is also important to enhance the players' **increased acceleration abilities through intensified training volume** and **larger scale game scenarios**.

3. Reaction Day

Engaging players in **cognitive challenges**, reaction day training sessions feature practices that demand **fast decision-making and adaptability**, without overly straining any particular physical attribute or muscle.

4. Pre-Match Activation Day

Tailored for pre-match preparation (the day before a match), the activation based warm up sessions **offer a break from intense physical demands**, creating a relaxed yet stimulating environment to maintain player enthusiasm and **minimise mental fatigue**.

Summary

By structuring warm up routines that seamlessly align with the physical and technical session objectives, coaches not only mitigate injury risks which may stem from insufficient preparation or lack of session progression, but also **enable the potential to foster a dynamic training atmosphere conducive to player development and maximise this time of the session across the training week**.

Additionally, by using a **variety of different warm ups in the sessions** throughout the weekly training cycle, coaches facilitate **continuous growth and adaptation**, laying the groundwork for **sustained improvement over time**. Ultimately, the integration of daily themed periodization principles into warm up routines serves to prime players and ready them for what will come next in the training flow, while reinforcing the holistic approach to player development endorsed by coaches at all levels of the game.

Benefits of the "Football Periodization" to Maximise Performance Methodology

Key Point

If the daily training content is poorly planned or managed with an insufficient methodological approach, poor performance occurs with the players insufficiently conditioned and significantly higher rates of injury.

What are the Recent Changes to Physical Preparation?

Individuals tasked with the development of football players have seen the understanding, progression and implementation of strength and conditioning, speed development and high-intensity football specific endurance training increase exponentially over the last 10-12 years. Furthermore, this has happened directly in accordance with growth in the players' tactical understanding of different systems of play.

What are the benefits?

- Enhancing the coaches' knowledge across a range of coaching and high-performance topics.
- Maximising the use of specific training games and practices in the training week (microcycle).
- Understanding the benefits of tapering strategies so that players arrive in optimal condition for competition.

Overall Picture of the Coaching Process

Maximising the physical profile and status of players is only a part of the performance target, as from a coach's perspective, building an integrated training process to a level where the physical, technical and tactical outcomes seamlessly fit into the development of the player or team, is fundamental to obtain performance progression within the coaching process.

Diagram Key

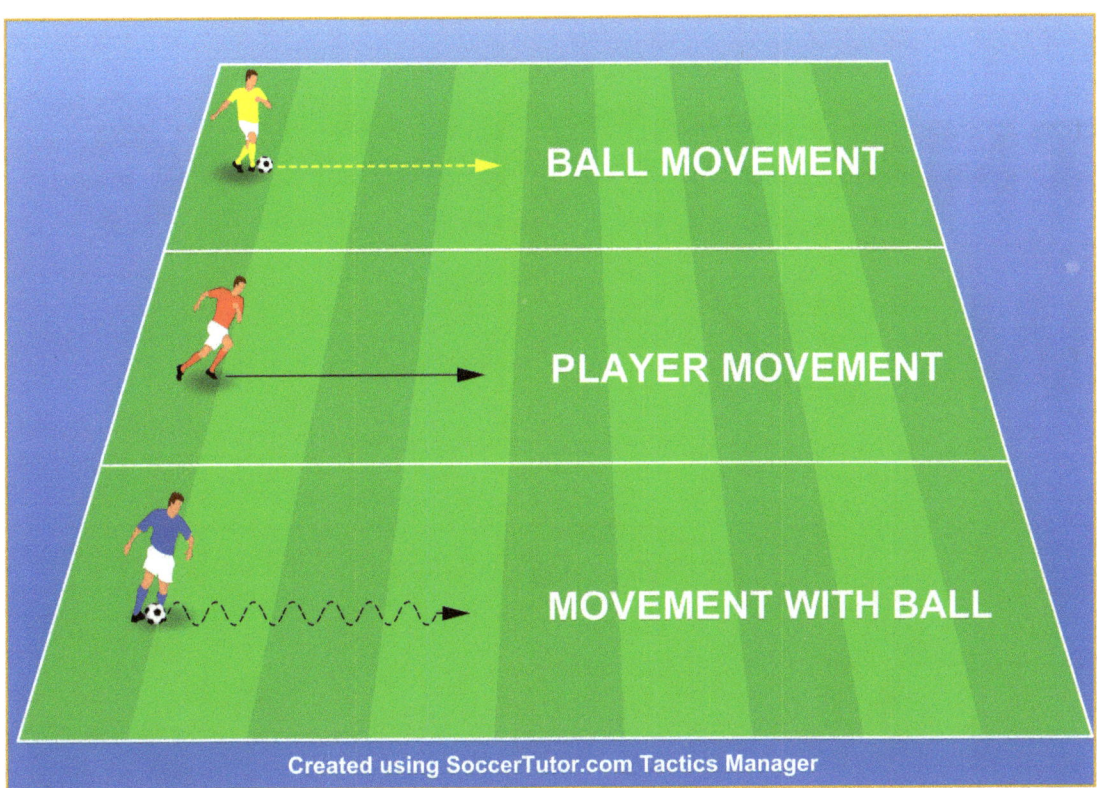

Practice Format

Each practice includes clear diagrams with supporting training notes:

- Name of Practice
- Practice Information and Data
- Objective of Practice
- Description of Practice
- Progressions and Coaching Points *(if applicable)*

The Training Week

THE TRAINING WEEK

The Training Week

Practice Design Considerations to Optimise Coaching Outcomes

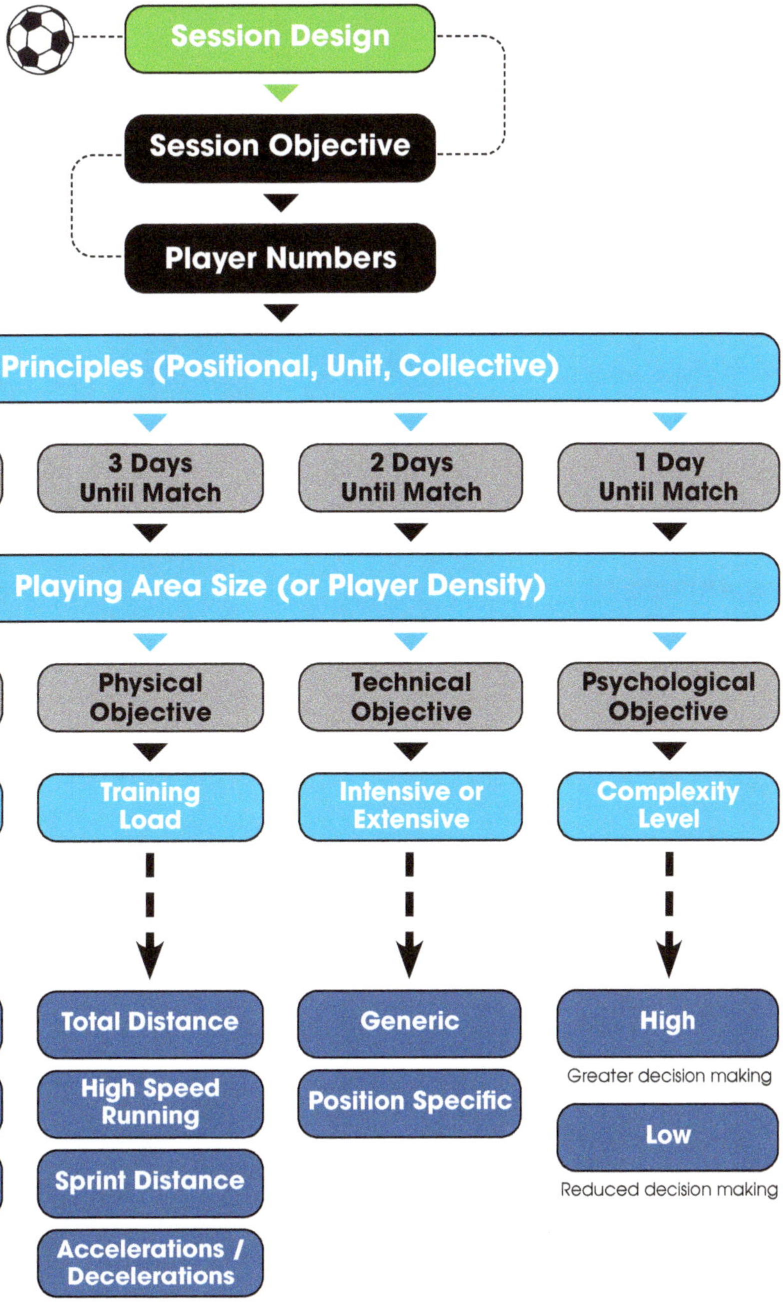

Session Design
↓
Session Objective
↓
Player Numbers
↓
Principles (Positional, Unit, Collective)

| 4 Days Until Match | 3 Days Until Match | 2 Days Until Match | 1 Day Until Match |

Playing Area Size (or Player Density)

| Tactical Objective | Physical Objective | Technical Objective | Psychological Objective |
| Game Phase Focus | Training Load | Intensive or Extensive | Complexity Level |

Attacking	Total Distance	Generic	High — *Greater decision making*
Defending	High Speed Running	Position Specific	Low — *Reduced decision making*
Transitions	Sprint Distance		
	Accelerations / Decelerations		

Warm Ups to Maximise Performance

The Training Week

Training Session Flow

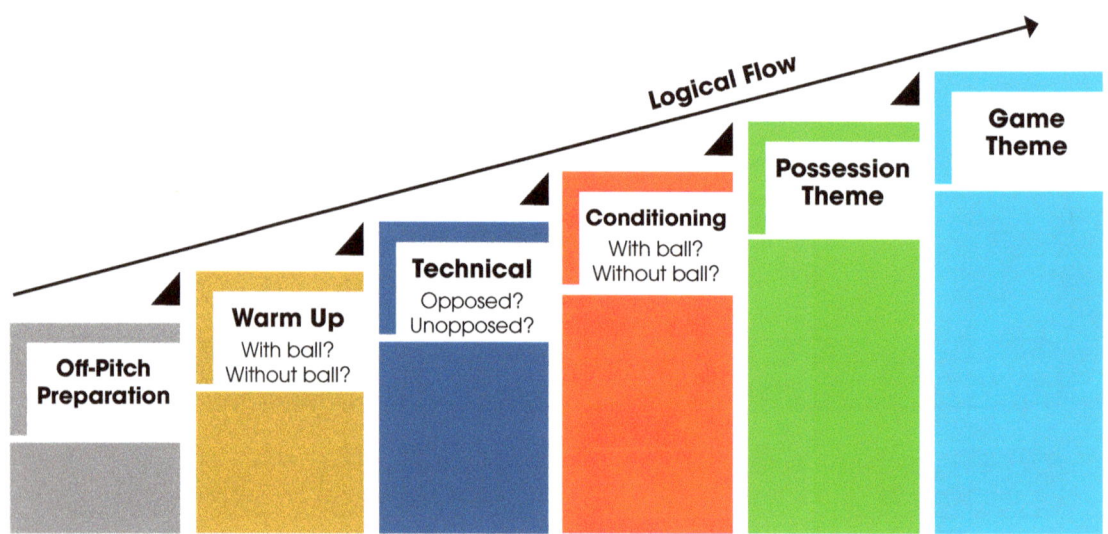

- Ensure logical flow through session – physical, technical, and tactical.
- Intelligent and efficient coaching – maintain focus and intensity.
- Be concise and direct with coaching points – maintain clarity.
- Use natural breaks to coach and get points across.
- Don't break the rhythm and reduce intensity.
- Sessions should flow!

Warm Up
- Don't just use as a time filler!
- Physically prepare for session demands.
- Psychological preparation (tactical).

Technical
- Continue flow of the session.
- Gradually increase intensity and demand from warm up phase.
- Influence technical, tactical, psychological and physical outcomes.
- Expansion or limitation of area size depending on physical requirements.

Conditioning
- Overload the physical focus of session.
- Induce key physical stimulus of session.
- Ensure opportunity for players to develop specific physical qualities.
- Prepare players fully for the upcoming intensity demands.

Possession
- Continue flow and demand of session.
- Ensure coaching within the phase is concise and intelligent, and match intensity achieves competition realism.
- Natural recovery breaks are key to minimise intensity/direction of session.

The Training Week

Planning the Training Week with Tapering Strategy to Maximise Performance

To assist in the practical application of the content, the flow of the training session is vitally important to increase the intensity, application and engagement of the players. This can be done through administering the content of the session through a logical flow, focusing on some simple key coaching points.

With good preparation, both tactically and physically, the players' roles and responsibilities can be understood further and lead to improved performances.

The following pages show you how to structure the training week (periodized microcycle) with a tapered strategy so your players can reach their peak performance.

Training week plans for Professional, Semi-professional, Youth Academy, and Grassroots (Youth) football are all included.

Periodized Practices to Maximise Performance has all different types of practices organised into their different sections:

- **Warm Up** (Resistance, Speed Endurance, Reaction Speed)
- **Technical** (Intensive, Extensive)
- **Conditioning** (Resistance, Speed Endurance, Reaction Speed)
- **Possession** (Small, Medium, Large)
- **Game** (Small, Medium, Large)

You can then drop these practice types into the applicable day and session on the training week session plans.

The Training Week

Practical Coaching Model to Build the Training Week (Microcycle)

This page often refers to the practices and physical data included in the Football Periodization to Maximise Performance book - please see pages 10-11 for full details.

The tables to follow provide a framework for coaches of various coaching levels or categories to utilise as a guide in order to structure their training week. Following this specific training methodology, it is possible to implement an integrated training concept. Being able to understand the physical, technical and tactical outcomes of the session are key to maximising the coaching time with the players involved.

Selecting from the various categorised practices in the Football Periodization book and the warm ups in this book in the correct order, it provides assistance with the fundamentally important session design phase. Furthermore, based on the understanding of the physical outcomes of each practice, coaches will be able to enhance their knowledge of how **the session design phase can be tailored to meet the session objectives from a physical, technical and tactical perspective**.

KEY POINT: Selection of practices in the two books (more volumes to follow soon) will generate a better understanding for coaches of the physical demands imposed by individual practices and accumulative total sessions over a period of time.

It should be noted that the physical data provided in the Football Periodization book practices has been generated from elite professional players, so it is suggested that practice durations, repetitions and area sizes are adapted to best suit the age groups being coached. The data values give the readers an understanding of the demands imposed on players at the level assessed. The physical output metrics are for coaches to understand how different practices can influence different physical loads.

The 5 different training week examples (microcycles) outlined on pages 20-25 are as follows:

1. **Professional Microcycle**
   (4 Training Sessions per week + Match + Compensatory Session)

2. **Semi-professional Microcycle**
   (3 Training Sessions per week + Match)

3. **Youth Academy Microcycle**
   (2 Training Sessions per week + Match)

4. **Grassroots (Youth) Microcycle 1 - Small Sided Game Focus**
   (1 Training Session per week, which alternates with Grassroots Microcycle 2)

5. **Grassroots (Youth) Microcycle 2 - Large Sided Game Focus**
   (1 Training Session per week, which alternates with Grassroots Microcycle 1)

The Training Week

Periodization, Tapering Strategy and Maximising Performance

The *Football Periodization to Maximise Performance Methodology* enables the development of a specific and integrated coaching approach to the training week, otherwise known as the **microcycle tapering strategy**.

It is well documented that placing various but contextual stressors on individual athletes or football players as a way of developing them from a physical, tactical and technical perspective is imperative. This is done through variation and changing of the training load but also ensuring the balance between work and recovery is apparent.

PERIODIZATION and TAPERING is a process of structuring and forward planning that involves the manipulation of key variables in order to cause a balanced approach to both overload and regeneration periods causing optimal performance (Mallo, 2015).

Manipulating key variables through **various constraints such as player numbers, surface area, training game types, bout duration, frequency and intensity, will significantly affect training load variables and outcomes, which conjunctively lead to performance enhancement** (Bosquet et al., 2007).

The strategy employed will be highlighted through **daily objectives or themes directly linked to their physiological focus**, whilst highlighting some of the key manipulated variables used to cause energy system and muscular overloads through football training concepts.

The practical coaching principles can be influenced by various game-model development or playing philosophies, and where possible, justify the content through published scientific work.

Please note that the training week (microcycle) overview is predominantly focusing on those starting players accumulating >45 to 60 minutes in competitive match-play.

Non-starters or squad players within the group obviously follow a program ensuring compensatory 'top-up' training is performed.

In order to understand the daily formatting, the content is titled by the number format of training days following the previous match (+), in addition to the number of days until the next fixture (-).

For example, in the Professional Microcycle (training week), the Tuesday training day is 3 days after the previous match and 4 days before the next match, so is therefore named **MD +3/-4**.

The Training Week

The Training Week:
Professional Microcycle

4 Training Sessions per Week + Match + Compensatory Session

DAY OF THE WEEK		MONDAY	TUESDAY	WEDNESDAY	THURSDAY	FRIDAY	SATURDAY	SUNDAY
Post-Game + / Pre-Game -		MD +2/-5	MD +3/-4	MD +4/-3	MD +5/-2	MD +6/-1	Match	MD +1/-6
Game Focus		Recovery	Intensive	Extensive	Balanced	Intensive	Extensive	Non-Starters
Tactical Focus		Evaluate	Defending	Attacking	Balanced	Review	Execute	-
PHYSICAL FOCUS		RECOVERY	RESISTANCE	SPEED END.	REACTION SPEED	ACTIVATION	MATCH	COMPEN-SATORY
Warm Up	Recovery	■						
	Resistance		■			■		
	Speed Endurance			■				
	Reaction Speed				■			
Technical	Intensive		■		■			
	Extensive			■				
Conditioning	Resistance		■					
	Speed Endurance			■				
	Reaction Speed				■	■		
Possession	Small Sided		■					
	Medium Sided				■			
	Large Sided			■				
Game	Small Sided		■					
	Medium Sided				■			
	Large Sided			■		■		

This example shows a specific methodology of work across the microcycle for professional or full-time training teams.

The Training Week

Training Session Format for Professional Microcycle

SUNDAY/MONDAY - 1/2 Days Until Match = Recovery

TUESDAY (70-75 min) - 4 Days Until Match (MD +3/-4)
Positional Principle Training and Resistance:

1. Resistance Warm Up (10-12 min)
2. Intensive Technical Practice (10-15 min)
3. Resistance Conditioning Practice (10-20 min)
4. Small Sided Possession (10-12 min)
5. Small Sided Game (10-25 min)

WEDNESDAY (85-95 min) - 3 Days Until Match (MD +4/-3)
Collective Team Principle Training and Speed Endurance:

1. Speed Endurance Warm Up (10-12 min)
2. Extensive Technical Practice (12-15 min)
3. Speed Endurance Conditioning Practice (5-15 min)
4. Large Sided Possession (10-15 min)
5. Large Sided Game in Large Area (10-50 min)

THURSDAY (60-70 min) - 2 Days Until Match (MD +5/-2)
Unit Principle Training and Reaction Speed Development:

1. Reaction Speed Warm Up (5-7 min)
2. Intensive Technical Practice (10-15 min)
3. Reaction Speed Conditioning Practice (5-15 min)
4. Medium Sided Possession (6-15 min)
5. Medium Sided Game (10-25 min)

FRIDAY (45-60 min) - 1 Day Until Match (MD +6/-1)
Pre-Match Activation Training Day:

1. Pre-Match Activation Warm Up (10-12 min)
2. Reaction Speed Conditioning Practice (5-15 min)
3. Large Sided Game in Small/Medium Area (10-50 min)

The Training Week

The Training Week:
Semi-Professional Microcycle

3 Training Sessions per Week + Match

DAY OF THE WEEK		MONDAY	TUESDAY	WEDNESDAY	THURSDAY	FRIDAY	SATURDAY	SUNDAY
Post-Game + / Pre-Game -		MD +2/-5	MD +3/-4	MD +4/-3	MD +5/-2	MD +6/-1	Match	MD +1/-6
Game Focus		Recovery	Intensive	Extensive	Recovery	Intensive	Extensive	Recovery
Tactical Focus		Free Evening	Defending	Attacking	Free Evening	Review	Execute	Free Evening
PHYSICAL FOCUS		RECOVERY	RESISTANCE	SPEED END.	RECOVERY	ACTIVATION	MATCH	RECOVERY
Warm Up	Recovery							
	Resistance		■			■		
	Speed Endurance			■				
	Reaction Speed							
Technical	Intensive		■					
	Extensive			■				
Conditioning	Resistance		■					
	Speed Endurance			■				
	Reaction Speed					■		
Possession	Small Sided		■					
	Medium Sided							
	Large Sided			■				
Game	Small Sided		■					
	Medium Sided						■	
	Large Sided			■				

This example shows a specific methodology of work across the microcycle for semi-professional teams training 3 times per week.

The Training Week

The Training Week:
Youth Academy Microcycle

2 Training Sessions per Week + Match

DAY OF THE WEEK		MONDAY	TUESDAY	WEDNESDAY	THURSDAY	FRIDAY	SATURDAY	SUNDAY
Post-Game + / Pre-Game -		MD +2/-5	MD +3/-4	MD +4/-3	MD +5/-2	MD +6/-1	Match	MD +1/-6
Game Focus		Recovery	Intensive	Recovery	Extensive	Recovery	Extensive	Recovery
Tactical Focus		Free Evening	Defending	Free Evening	Attacking	Free Evening	Execute	Free Evening
PHYSICAL FOCUS		RECOVERY	RESISTANCE	RECOVERY	SPEED END.	RECOVERY	MATCH	RECOVERY
Warm Up	Recovery							
	Resistance		■					
	Speed Endurance				■			
	Reaction Speed							
Technical	Intensive		■					
	Extensive				■			
Conditioning	Resistance		■					
	Speed Endurance				■			
	Reaction Speed							
Possession	Small Sided		■					
	Medium Sided							
	Large Sided				■			
Game	Small Sided		■					
	Medium Sided							
	Large Sided				■			

This example shows a specific methodology of work across the microcycle for youth academy teams training 2 times per week.

The Training Week

The Training Week:
Grassroots (Youth) Microcycle 1

SSG/Resistance Focus - Alternates with Grassroots (Youth) Microcycle 2

DAY OF THE WEEK		MONDAY	TUESDAY	WEDNESDAY	THURSDAY	FRIDAY	SATURDAY	SUNDAY
Post-Game + / Pre-Game -		MD +2/-5	MD +3/-4	MD +4/-3	MD +5/-2	MD +6/-1	Match	MD +1/-6
Game Focus		Recovery	Intensive	Extensive	Balanced	Intensive	Extensive	Non-Starters
Tactical Focus		Evaluate	Defending	Attacking	Balanced	Review	Execute	-
PHYSICAL FOCUS		RECOVERY	RESISTANCE	SPEED END.	REACTION SPEED	ACTIVATION	MATCH	COMPENSATORY
Warm Up	Recovery	■						
	Resistance		■			■		
	Speed Endurance			■				
	Reaction Speed				■			
Technical	Intensive		■					
	Extensive			■				
Conditioning	Resistance		■					
	Speed Endurance			■				
	Reaction Speed				■	■		
Possession	Small Sided	■						
	Medium Sided				■			
	Large Sided			■				
Game	Small Sided		■					
	Medium Sided						■	
	Large Sided			■		■		

Grassroots (Youth) Microcycle 1 has a small sided game focus and alternates with Grassroots (Youth) Microcycle 2 - <u>see next page</u>, which has a large sided game focus.

The Training Week

The Training Week:
Grassroots (Youth) Microcycle 2

LSG/Speed Endurance Focus - Alternates with Grassroots (Youth) Microcycle 1

DAY OF THE WEEK		MONDAY	TUESDAY	WEDNESDAY	THURSDAY	FRIDAY	SATURDAY	SUNDAY
Post-Game + / Pre-Game -		MD +2/-5	MD +3/-4	MD +4/-3	MD +5/-2	MD +6/-1	Match	MD +1/-6
Game Focus		Recovery	Recovery	Extensive	Recovery	Recovery	Extensive	Recovery
Tactical Focus		Free Evening	Free Evening	Defending	Free Evening	Free Evening	Execute	Free Evening
PHYSICAL FOCUS		RECOVERY	RECOVERY	SPEED END.	RECOVERY	RECOVERY	MATCH	RECOVERY
Warm Up	Recovery							
	Resistance							
	Speed Endurance			■				
	Reaction Speed							
Technical	Intensive							
	Extensive			■				
Conditioning	Resistance							
	Speed Endurance			■				
	Reaction Speed							
Possession	Small Sided							
	Medium Sided							
	Large Sided			■				
Game	Small Sided							
	Medium Sided							
	Large Sided			■				

Grassroots (Youth) Microcycle 2 has a large sided game focus and alternates with Grassroots (Youth) Microcycle 1 - <u>see previous page</u>, which has a small sided game focus.

The Training Week

Analysis of a 6-Week Training Mesocycle and Positional Quantification in Elite European Football Players

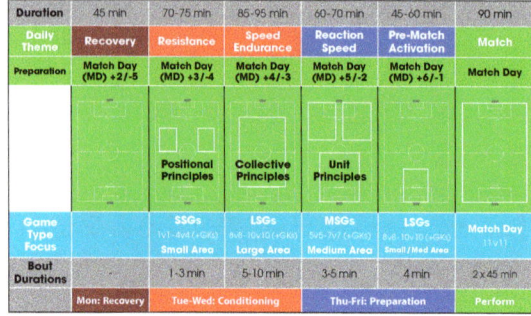

 What?

Analyse a training mesocycle whilst quantifying positional demands imposed on elite European football players.

 When?

Data recorded from players across a 6-week in-season training mesocycle period.

 How?

- Daily **GPS** and **rating of perceived exertion (RPE)** load recorded.
- Metrics included: **Total distance** (m), **high-intensity distance** (m), **sprint distance** (m), **average speed** (m.min), **RPE load** (RPE x duration).
- **Positional demands** and **training loads** analysed in addition with match conditions (i.e. match location and match score), as well as player's age.

 Who?

16 elite male European football players participated in the study.

 Results?

- **Training Loads:** Typical daily training loads did not differ throughout each week of the in-season mesocycle. Total Load (TL) significantly reduced on MD-1 vs. TLs on MD-2, MD-3 and MD-4 preceding a match.
- Physical output differences found between MD-2, MD-3, and MD-4 revealed a structured, tapering approach to microcycle.
- **Positional: WFs =>** Total distance and Very High Intensity Running (VHIR) distance vs. other positions; **CBs** = significantly less < Total Distance (TD) and VHIR vs. other positions.
- Reduced average speeds (metres per min) reported in training sessions post-successful matches vs. post-defeats (p<0.05).
- Reduced average speeds (metres per min) also reported post-away fixtures vs. home fixtures within the microcycle.

Practical Application?

- Coaches can maintain a uniformed and structured training load mesocycle whilst inducing variation of the physical outputs during the microcycle phase.
- Additionally, the investigation also provides a tapering approach that may induce significant variation of the positional demands.

Full Scientific Reference

Owen AL., Lago-Penas C., Gomez AM., Mendes B., Delial A. (2017). Analysis of a Training Mesocycle & Positional Quantification in Elite European Soccer Players | International Journal of Sport Science & Coaching, DOI: 10.1177/1747954117727851

PERIODIZATION OF WARM UPS

Periodization of Warm Ups

Scientific Research

In modern football, the warm up is often overlooked, but it should be viewed as a crucial training phase.

Periodizing the warm up throughout the training microcycle (training week) and day can maximise player time and optimise subsequent training responses. **Coaches can gain a big advantage by creatively utilising the 10-15 minutes of daily warm up time.**

Active warm ups enhance muscle temperature, nerve conductivity, and metabolic reactions, with added benefits like increased blood flow and post-activation potentiation (PAP), which is when there is improvement in performance as a result of using a conditioning exercise (Zois et al., 2011).

Recent research challenges traditional warm ups, suggesting how mirroring team sports' movement and metabolic demands in warm ups can achieve higher intensity in less time. Extended warm ups (>30 min) may negatively impact performance and psychological readiness (Romaratezabala et al., 2018), and player motivation. Studies propose dedicating 5–10 minutes to activities at 40–70% of maximal oxygen consumption for optimal performance markers, whilst also showing that sprint-based activities in warm ups enhance running speed and overall performance (Zois et al., 2011).

Warm Ups With or Without a Ball?

A well-designed warm up serves as a bridge between a player's current state and the training challenges. Incorporating the ball engages players cognitively, stimulating technical demands. However, for variability, coaches should also choose warm ups without the ball in order to focus on specific physical movements, especially at the elite level.

Dynamic Warm Ups to Best Prepare for the Training Session

It has been proposed that dynamic warm ups which replicate the upcoming activity movements enhance performance by increasing muscle excitability, which can be extremely valuable for coaches. This suggests that such **exercises prepare muscles for directional changes, sprints, and jumping efforts** (Guinoubi et al., 2015). Understanding muscles and energy systems is crucial for all coaches working in team sports like football, as **incorporating dynamic stretching, mobility exercises, and specific drills, with or without the ball, readies players physically and mentally for subsequent practices, enhancing performance and reducing the risk of injury** (Owen et al., 2013).

The warm up should address energy systems and specific muscles that players will use in training. Integrating progressive heart rate increments and mimicking football's intermittent nature with high-intensity bursts and recovery periods prepares players for upcoming challenges (Owen et al., 2011; Bangsbo, 1994).

Periodization of Warm Ups

General Warm Up Exercises Without the Ball Movement Examples

Source: Adapted from research by Taylor et al., (2009).

Exercise	Duration
01. High knees	• 3 Sets x 20m
02. Butt flicks	• 3 Sets x 20m
03. Carioca (samba)	• 3 Sets x 20m (on each side)
04. Dynamic hamstring swings	• 10 x Reps (on each leg)
05. Dynamic groin swings	• 10 x Reps (on each leg)
06. Arm swings: Forward & backward	• 10 x Reps (in each direction)
07. Faster high knees (shorter stride)	• 4 Sets x 10m
08. Swerving	• 2 Sets x 30m (at 70% of max speed)
09. Side stepping	• 2 Sets x 30m (at 80% of max speed)
10. Spider-man walks	• 1 Set x 20m
11. Sideways low squat walks	• 1 Set x 10 Steps (in each direction)
12. Upper body rotations	• 10 Reps (on each leg)
13. Vertical jump	• 5 Reps (building in intensity)
14. Run through	• 2 Sets x 20m (at 70% max speed) • 2 Sets x 20m (at 80% max speed) • 1 Set x 20m (at 90% max speed)
15. Counter-movement jump, then 5m Sprint	• 2 Sets x 5m (at 90% max speed) • 1 Set x 5m (at 95% max speed)
16. 5m Sprint, then counter-movement jump	• 2 Sets x 5m

Periodization of Warm Ups

Considerations of the Microcycle (Training Week)

Working to a specific coaching strategy or following a specific training microcycle, which encompasses numerous sessions within a week, demands a strategic and well-balanced approach. **Crafting tailored warm up routines aligned with the specific physical, technical, and psychological goals of each particular training session creates a real training flow, precision, variability, and injury prevention focus.**

As detailed in the *"Football Periodization" book (see pages 10-11 for details)* methodology, the key lies in aligning the right warm up sessions on the right days in order to optimise fitness levels and ensure player readiness.

At the outset of the week, especially when players are more recovered and gearing up for more intensive and extensive practices, the focus shifts from gentle mobility exercises and light ball work to more demanding and customised warm up activities.

As the week unfolds and training intensity escalates, the warm up should evolve, gradually escalating to match the demands of the daily training sessions and physical themes. This thoughtful progression serves not only to enhance performance but also contributes to maintaining the players' freshness throughout the training cycle.

Periodized Training Days in the Planned Training Week

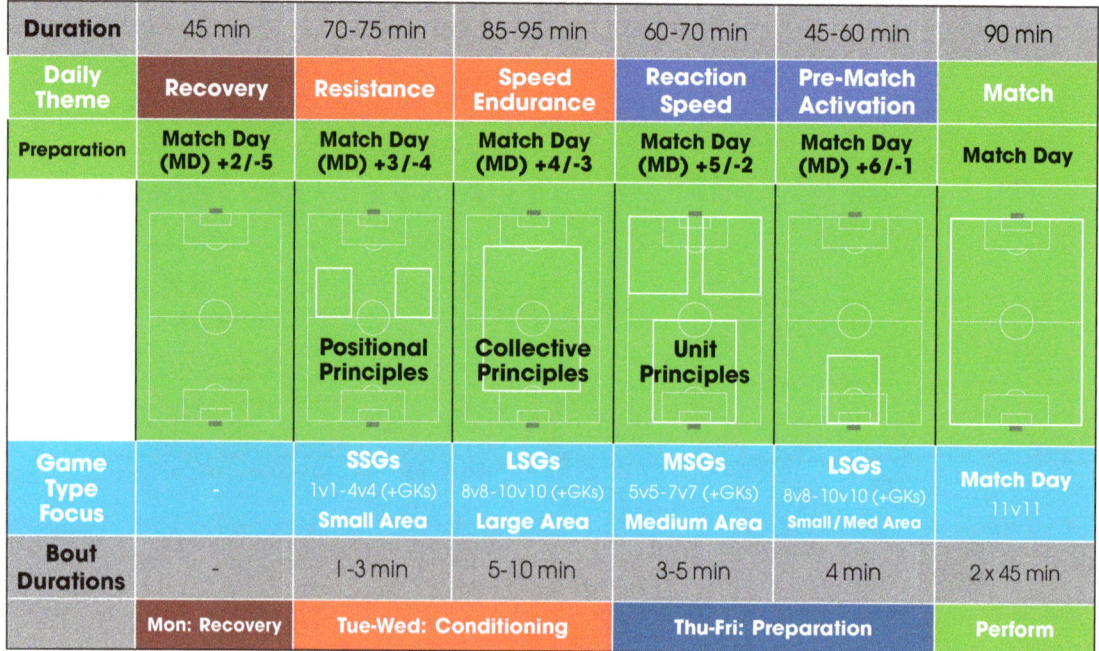

Duration	45 min	70-75 min	85-95 min	60-70 min	45-60 min	90 min
Daily Theme	Recovery	Resistance	Speed Endurance	Reaction Speed	Pre-Match Activation	Match
Preparation	Match Day (MD) +2/-5	Match Day (MD) +3/-4	Match Day (MD) +4/-3	Match Day (MD) +5/-2	Match Day (MD) +6/-1	Match Day
		Positional Principles	Collective Principles	Unit Principles		
Game Type Focus	-	SSGs 1v1-4v4 (+GKs) Small Area	LSGs 8v8-10v10 (+GKs) Large Area	MSGs 5v5-7v7 (+GKs) Medium Area	LSGs 8v8-10v10 (+GKs) Small/Med Area	Match Day 11v11
Bout Durations	-	1-3 min	5-10 min	3-5 min	4 min	2 x 45 min
	Mon: Recovery	Tue-Wed: Conditioning		Thu-Fri: Preparation		Perform

Periodization of Warm Ups

Progressive Intensity

Progressive Intensity is a key warm up principle for all players, emphasising a gradual increase in effort to replicate game demands.

Regardless of age or level, abrupt shifts from rest to high intensity can disrupt aerobic systems, increase the risk of injury, and compromise performance.

Well-executed warm ups prevent or limit the rate of oxygen debt (as shown below in the diagram), and this is crucial in extended team sports like football, as substitutions and re-starting the second half can have a direct impact on physical performance outcomes, and potential results.

Therefore, this should be considered when planning a pre-match warm up or making substitutions during a game (Hills et al., 2019; Edholm et al., 2015; Fashioni et al., 2020).

When preparing the flow of the warm up, starting the training session with lower level intensity activities and movement mechanics, whilst gradually incorporating faster dynamic agility drills (with or without the ball) from the beginning ensures players are **mentally and physically prepared for the challenges ahead without causing elevated injury risk or negative psychological emotions**.

Reducing the Impact of Oxygen Debt

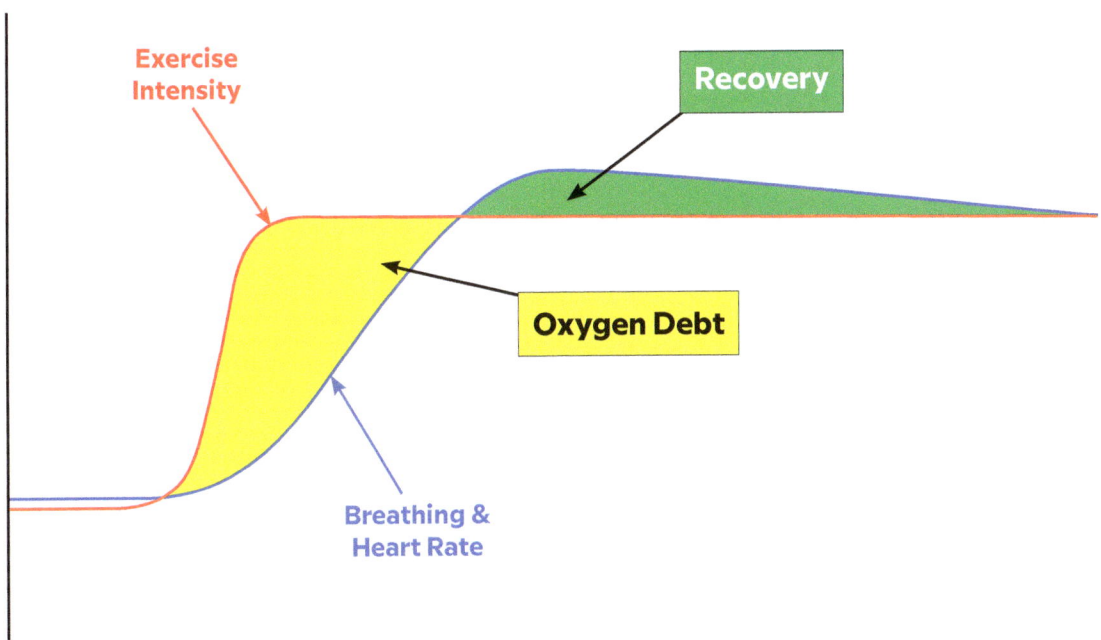

Periodization of Warm Ups

Scientific Research

While continuous research delves into this field, further investigations surrounding the topic are imperative to gain profound insights into the ideal warm up strategy for players, **ensuring their physical readiness for peak performance without inducing undue fatigue**.

Until essential information regarding this facet of training and match preparation is obtained, coaches should approach warm ups strategically, relying on experience and adhering to sensible best practices to yield positive outcomes. **Across all levels and abilities of the game, optimising training time with the players is fundamental, so being creative with warm ups is crucial**. For younger age groups, coaches may emphasise technical development through activities like rotational passing drills and passing games. In contrast, with older players, a gradual approach to prepare for the session's intensity is preferred, incorporating dynamic flexibility actions.

The key lies in aligning warm ups with specific training session requirements, focusing on relevant muscles and energy systems, and adapting across the training cycle. This comprehensive approach enhances both physical and mental readiness across different player levels.

Walker (2024) notes the historical emphasis on **2 Warm Up Objectives** in recreational football:

1. Mental preparation
2. Physical preparation

In recent times, warm ups are recognised for **4 Essential Purposes**:

1. Mental Readiness
2. Physical Readiness
3. Injury Prevention
4. Performance Enhancement

Progression of Warm Ups in Professional Football Training

In professional football environments, warm ups have evolved into a standard practice addressing these critical aspects, resulting in **improved performance and reduced injury risks**. The traditional 2 minute jog and static stretching have given way to contemporary methodologies, **incorporating the latest knowledge in sports science**. This shift reflects a strategic re-evaluation of player performance strategies in elite environments.

Components of a Good Generalised and Preventive Warm Up

By Donald T Kirkendall PhD., Aspetar Journal of Sport Medicine, 2014.

- **Strengthen Areas Known to be a Problem**
- **Light Running Exercises**
- **Dynamic Flexibility**
- **Motor Control Activities**
- **Static & Dynamic Balance**
- **Plyometrics**
- **Agility Work**

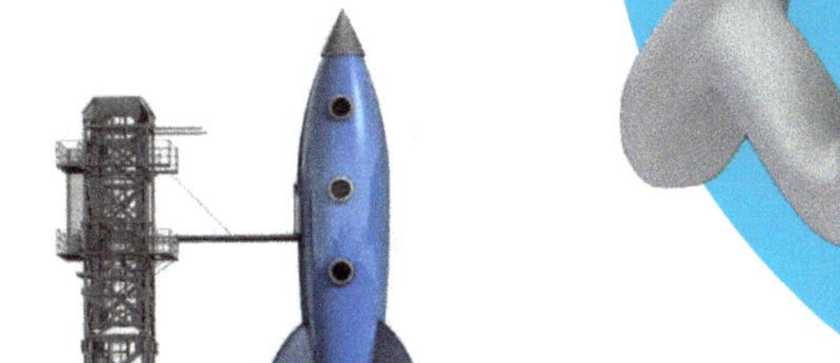

* Check the 11 + FIFA's Generalised Warm Up Program for a 15-20min applied example.

RESISTANCE WARM UPS

Resistance Warm Ups

Resistance Warm Up Practices

Based on the principles set out in the **"Football Periodization" book (see pages 10-11 for details)**, this section of the book emphasises the importance of "resistance" based warm ups.

Applied on **days involving high-intensity movements**, this strategic warm up incorporates external forces during **accelerations**, **decelerations**, and **changes of direction**. The controlled resistance pushes muscles beyond their usual range, activating the neuromuscular system to prepare the body for the subsequent high-intensity training demands.

Strategic Implementation
Smaller Based Density Training Preparation

The deliberate application of resistance based warm ups is highlighted, especially on days when training is centred around **dynamic explosive actions and movements**, coupled with the unpredictable nature ingrained in the game. Typically conducted on days with reduced playing densities or **smaller pitch dimensions**, these warm up sessions prepare players for drills/practices involving quick accelerations to outpace opponents, sudden decelerations, and directional changes essential in strategic plays. This ensures players are physically prepared for the specific challenges they are about to encounter.

Impact on Muscle Groups
1. Adductor Muscles

Resistance warm ups intentionally target adductor muscles, crucial for handling the strain imposed by frequent lateral movements in football.

Weekly inclusion readies the muscles for session demands, providing conditioning over time and reducing the risk of strains during lateral activities.

2. Abductors Muscles

External force resistance engages the abductors, promoting stability and strength needed for balance during rapid directional changes.

Resistance warm ups serve as a vital tool, stimulating abductor muscles and contributing to their conditioning over time for on-pitch challenges.

3. Quadricep Muscles (Quads)

Quads play a vital role in football, particularly in explosive movements, evasive actions, and technical striking. Additional load on specific training days acts as an overload stimulus, prompting swift adaptation to increased demand.

Summary

The resistance based warm ups presented in this book and throughout the **"Football Periodization" book methodology (see pages 10-11 for details)** is a dynamic and strategic approach to physical preparation in football. Deliberately targeting and controlling the overload in specific muscle groups, coaches not only provide players the chance to adapt and **link specific actions towards the forthcoming high-intensity demands, optimise on-pitch performance**, but they also act over time as a way of providing **additional conditioning stimulus and assist in the reduction of injuries**, which is crucial for success.

Resistance Warm Ups

Effects of Cutting Technique Modification on Change of Direction Performance

27 Multi-directional Male Athletes were Distributed into 2 Groups:

CONTROL GROUP  VS **EXPERIMENTAL GROUP**

Normal training

Two 30-minute change of direction speed and technique modification sessions per week with externally directed verbal coaching cueing (45° and 90°).

"Slam on the brakes."
"Cushion & push the ground away."
"Face towards direction of travel."

RESULTS

1. Change of direction speed and technique modification resulted in improvements in cutting performance, which were meaningfully greater than the control group.

2. The positive improvements in cutting performance were primarily attributed to increases in velocity at key instances of the penultimate foot contact and final foot contact, increases in propulsive force over shorter ground contact times, and reduced knee flexion.

Change of direction speed and technique modification is a simple, effective training method requiring minimal equipment that can enhance change of direction performance, which practitioners should consider incorporating into their training programs.

Reference: Dos'Santos et al. JSCR 2022   *Designed by @YLMSportScience*

Resistance Warm Ups

4 DAYS UNTIL MATCH (MD +3/-4)
Positional Principles and Resistance

Duration	45 min	70-75 min	85-95 min	60-70 min	45-60 min	90 min
Daily Theme	Recovery	RESISTANCE	Speed Endurance	Reaction Speed	Pre-Match Activation	Match
Preparation	Match Day (MD) +2/-5	Match Day (MD) +3/-4	Match Day (MD) +4/-3	Match Day (MD) +5/-2	Match Day (MD) +6/-1	Match Day
		Positional Principles	Collective Principles	Unit Principles		
Game Type Focus	-	SSGs 1v1-4v4 (+GKs) Small Area	LSGs 8v8-10v10 (+GKs) Large Area	MSGs 5v5-7v7 (+GKs) Medium Area	LSGs 8v8-10v10 (+GKs) Small/Med Area	Match Day 11v11
Bout Durations	-	1-3 min	5-10 min	3-5 min	4 min	2 x 45 min
	Mon: Recovery	Tue-Wed: Conditioning		Thu-Fri: Preparation		Perform

* **Training Week based on Professional Microcycle Example** - see pages 20-21.

Key Focus on:
- **Positional Principles**
- **Higher Muscle Resistance**
- **Changes of Direction** (CODs)
- **Accelerations and Decelerations** (A:D)

Resistance Warm Ups

RESISTANCE TRAINING SESSION
4 Days Until Match (MD +3/-4)

Positional Principle Training and Resistance (70-75 min):

1. Resistance Warm Up (10-12 min)
2. Intensive Technical Practice (10-15 min)
3. Resistance Conditioning Practice (10-20 min)
4. Small Sided Possession (10-12 min)
5. Small Sided Game (10-25 min)

Resistance Warm Ups

4 DAYS UNTIL MATCH (MD +3/-4)
Resistance Warm Up Practices

INTENSITY: All practices are performed at full intensity

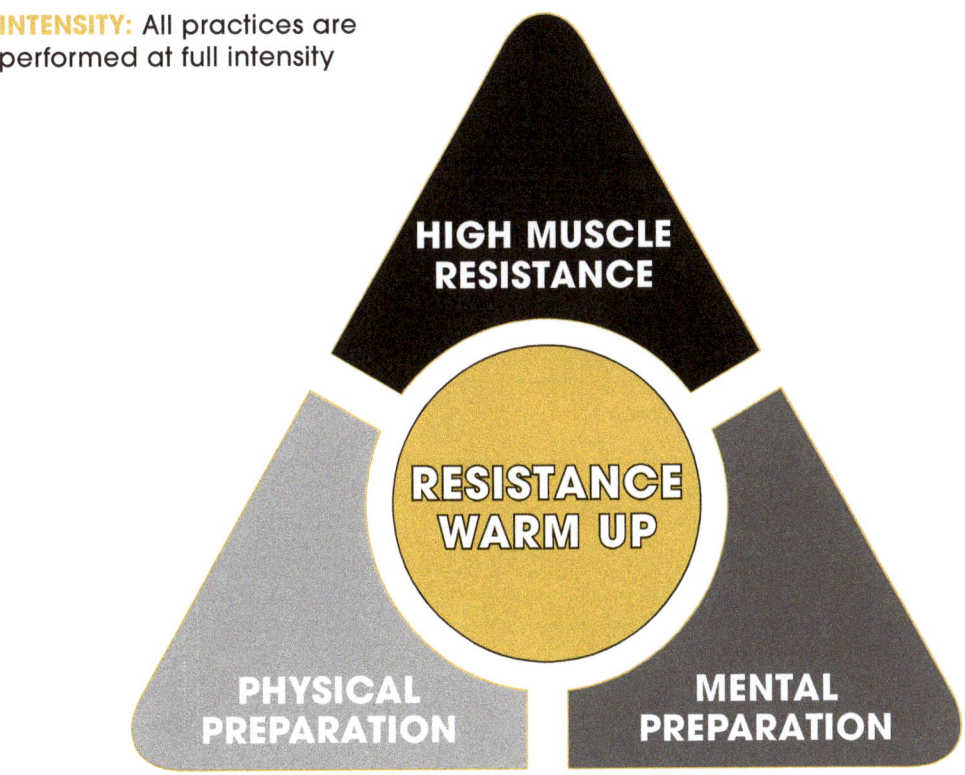

What are Resistance Warm Ups?
- Include many stop and start actions, directional changes, lower level accelerations, and decelerations in tight spaces.
- Activate the muscle groups for the explosive maximum accelerations and decelerations later in the session.
- Provide resistance to the working muscles through explosive actions in small spaces.

Why are they used on this day of the training week (MD +3/-4)?
- To prepare the players for the smaller surface area type work developed through the course of the session.

How does this help to maximise performance?
- Resistance warm ups are used on this day as a way of preparing the players muscles used for changing directions, acceleration and deceleration efforts.
- Resistance warm ups also generally ready the body for the session ahead (small sided games).

Resistance Warm Ups

Resistance 1. Agility, Coordination, and Balance Hurdle Exercises Warm Up Circuit

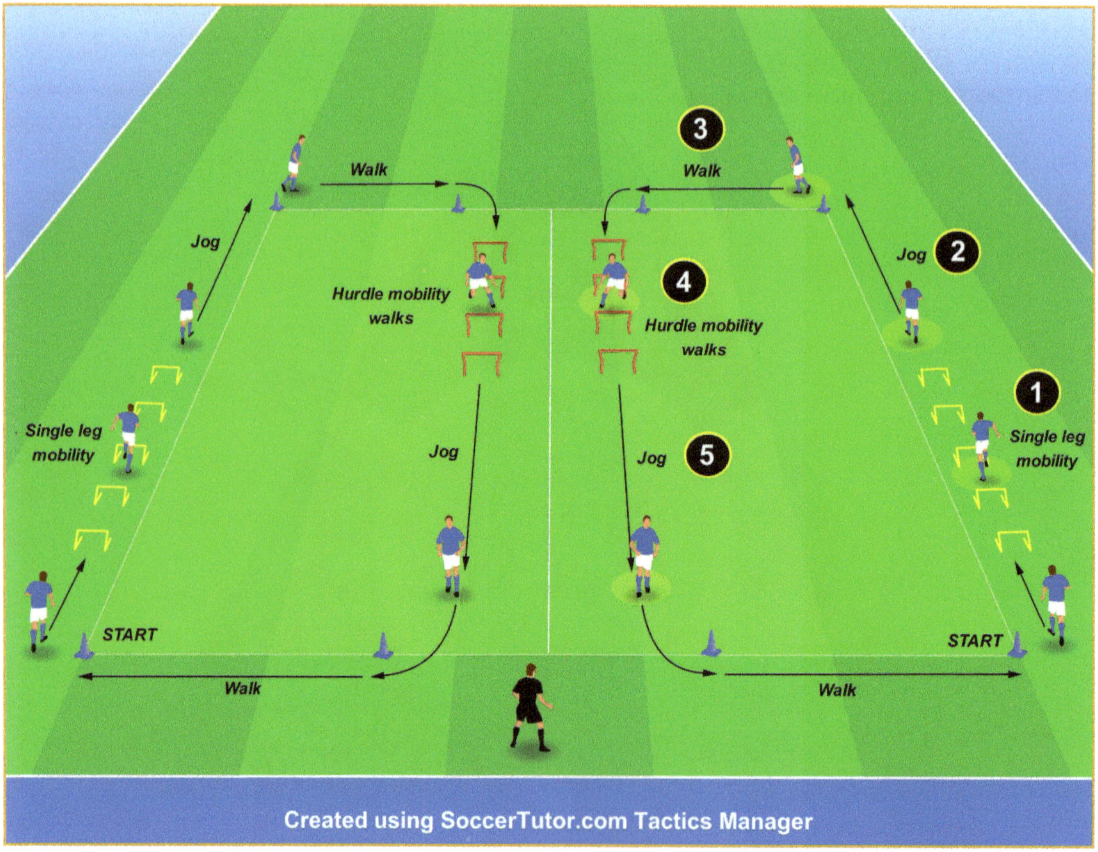

Duration	Reps	Sets	Numbers	Size (m)	Work Duration
5-10 min	2-3 min	3-4	Groups of 6-10	20 x 5	5-10 min

OBJECTIVE: Agility, balance, speed, flexibility, strength, and power.

The players all work in groups and go one behind the other in a continuous circuit:

1. Single leg mobility (hopping) through the 5 yellow hurdles.
2. Jog to first cone.
3. Walk to second cone.
4. Hurdle mobility walks through the 4 red hurdles.
5. Jog to final cone and walk to start position.

Resistance Warm Ups

Resistance 2. Speed, Coordination, and Power Exercises 4-Station Warm Up Circuit

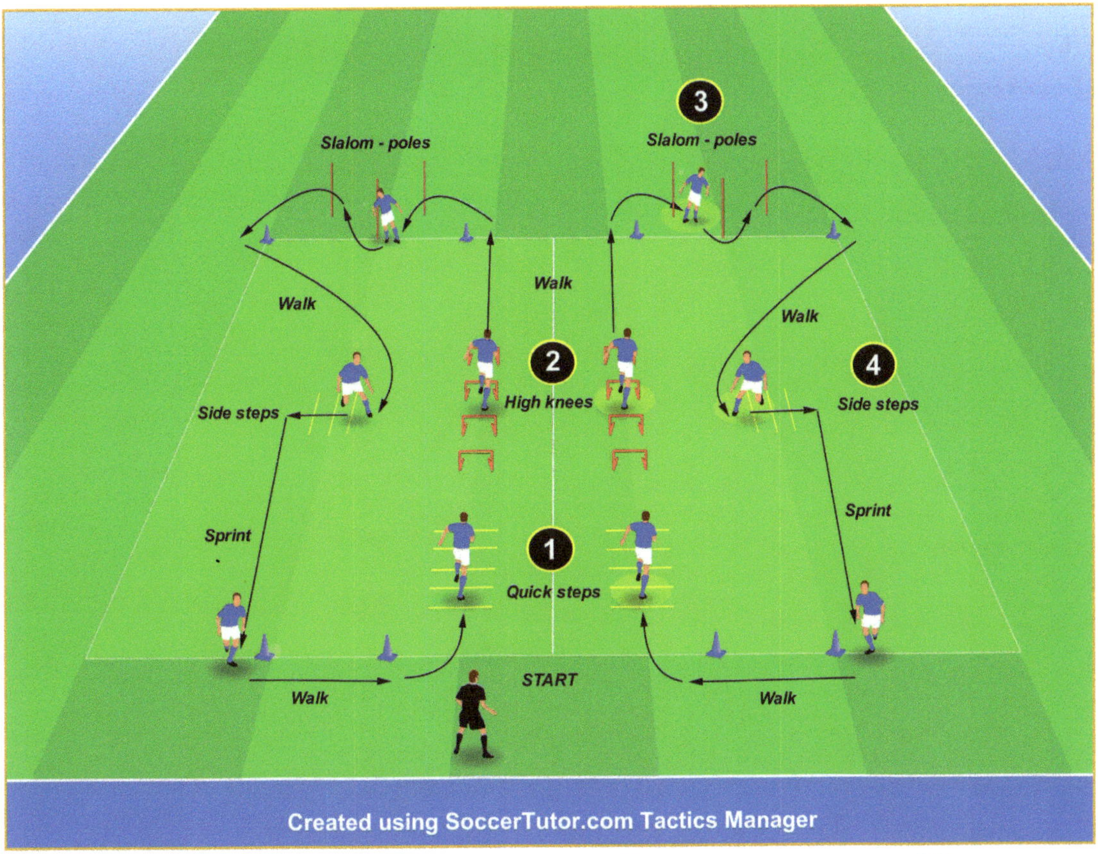

Duration	Reps	Sets	Numbers	Size (m)	Work Duration
10 min	4-4-4-4	3	4-20	30 x 30	5-6 min

OBJECTIVE: Explosive power and speed exercises to prepare for resistance session.

The players complete 4 reps at each station before moving to the next station in the circuit. They walk in between the stations.

1. Quick steps through the 5 ground poles across 10m distance (4 x reps).
2. High knees through the 4 hurdles across 10m distance (4 x reps).
3. Slalom run through the 3 poles across 10m distance (4 x reps).
4. Side steps through 3 ground poles + 15m sprint to cone (4 x reps).

Warm Ups to Maximise Performance

Resistance Warm Ups

Resistance 3. Coordination, Lateral Movement, and Quick Reactions Warm Up

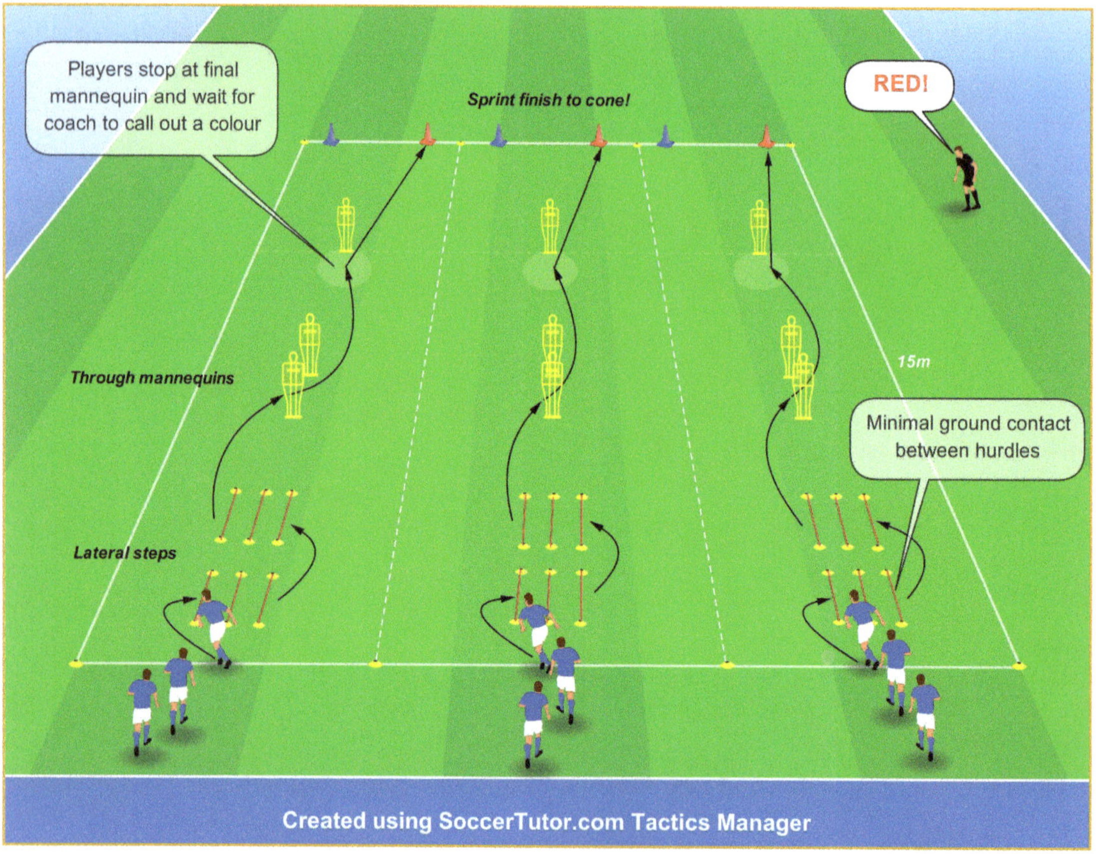

Duration	Reps	Sets	Numbers	Size (m)	Work Duration
10 min	4	3-4	Groups of 3-5	15 Length	8-10 min

OBJECTIVE: Agility coordination, quick reactions, and acceleration/speed.

- In groups (channels), the players perform lateral steps over the first 3 low ground hurdles and repeat for the next 3 ground hurdles. They then run through the first 2 mannequins before stopping at the third.

- The coach calls out "**Red**" or "**Blue**," and the players sprint to that colour cone.

COACHING POINTS:

1. Start with general warm up without explosive movements and gradually build intensity and speed.

2. Ensure players stop before reacting to the colour called out + have quick reactions to the colour called!

Resistance Warm Ups

Resistance 4. The "Mirror" Technical Ball Control in Grids Warm Up

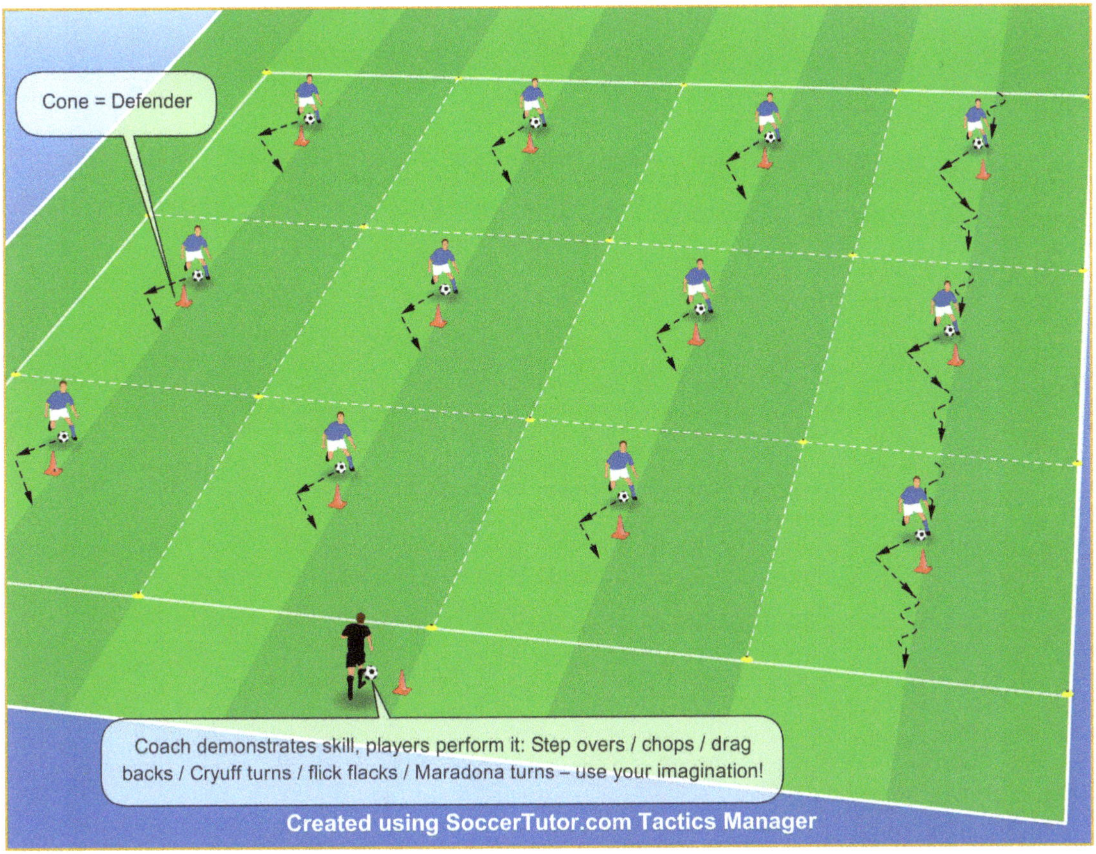

Cone = Defender

Coach demonstrates skill, players perform it: Step overs / chops / drag backs / Cryuff turns / flick flacks / Maradona turns – use your imagination!

Created using SoccerTutor.com Tactics Manager

Duration	Reps	Sets	Numbers	Size (m)	Work Duration
5-10 min	10-12	10	1-12	5 x 5 Squares	5-6 min

OBJECTIVE: Technical skills versus defender within a light warm up exercise.

- All of the players stand within their own grid with a ball each.
- The coach demonstrates a skill and dictates to the players when and what to do. The players then perform the skills at the same time as each other (synchronised).
- Use the cones as a focal point (defender) in which to perform the skill around/past.
- The 10 sets/skills include step overs, chops, drag backs, Cruyff turns, Maradona turns, etc. Alternatively, allow the players to use their imagination.

Warm Ups to Maximise Performance

Resistance Warm Ups

Resistance 5. The "Guantlet" Technical Ball Control and Moves to Beat Defenders Warm Up

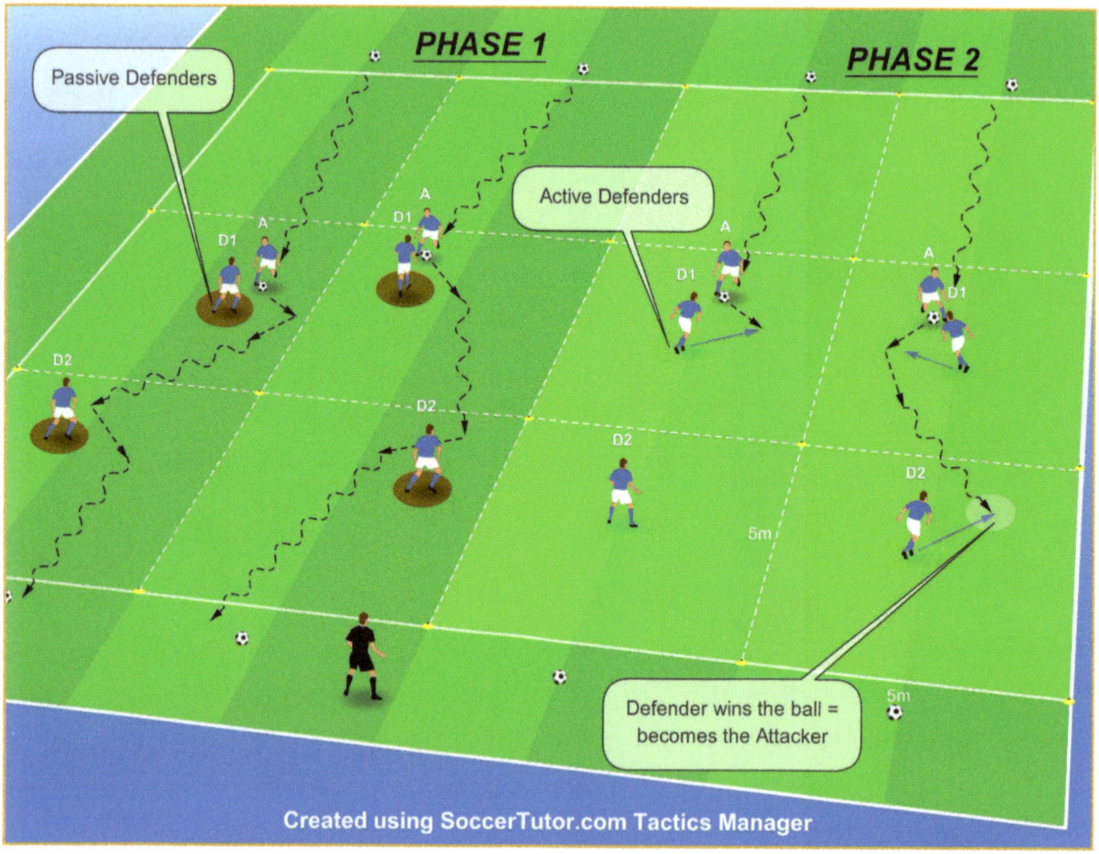

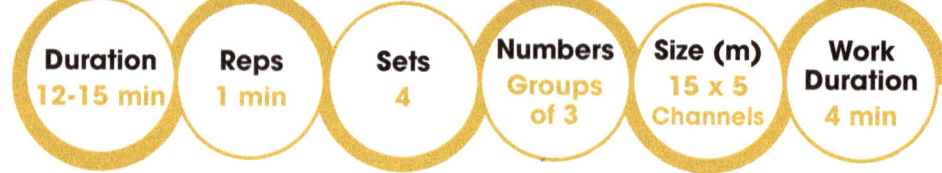

Duration	Reps	Sets	Numbers	Size (m)	Work Duration
12-15 min	1 min	4	Groups of 3	15 x 5 Channels	4 min

OBJECTIVE: Technical ball control, dribbling, and moves to beat defenders.

- The players are in groups of 3 within channels which have 3 grids.
- **Player A** starts outside and dribbles towards the first passive defender in the middle grid (**D1**).
- **Player A** performs skills to beat both defenders (**D1 + D2**) and dribble to end.
- **Player A** then repeats the same in the opposite direction (4 total).
- The coach rotates the roles to ensure all players have a turn at beating the 2 defenders.
- **PROGRESSION:** The defenders become active and try to win the ball.

Resistance Warm Ups

Resistance 6. Close Ball Control Skills Through Poles "Ronaldinho" Warm Up Circuit

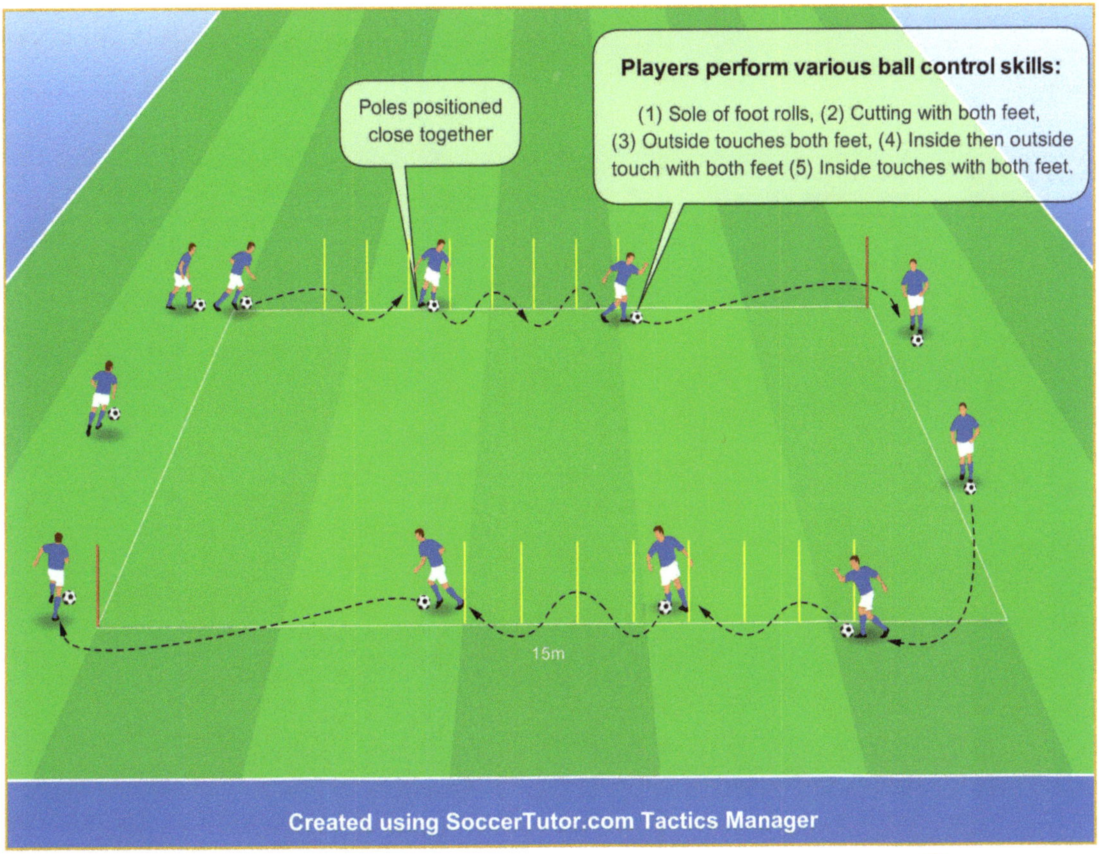

Poles positioned close together

Players perform various ball control skills:
(1) Sole of foot rolls, (2) Cutting with both feet, (3) Outside touches both feet, (4) Inside then outside touch with both feet (5) Inside touches with both feet.

15m

Created using SoccerTutor.com Tactics Manager

Duration	Reps	Sets	Numbers	Size (m)	Work Duration
5-10 min	1 Circuit	10	Groups	15 x 10	5-10 min

OBJECTIVE: Close ball control and dribbling technique with all parts of the foot.

In this circuit, the players move through the poles which are positioned close together. The players perform different ball control skills for each rep of the circuit, such as:

- Left or right foot only.
- Alternate feet.
- Sole of the foot rolls (single or both feet).
- "Cutting" touches with both feet.
- Outside touches with both feet.
- Inside touch, then outside touch with both feet.
- Inside touches with both feet.

Resistance Warm Ups

Resistance 7. Lateral Speed of Movement and Ball Skills Dynamic Zig-Zag Warm Up Circuit

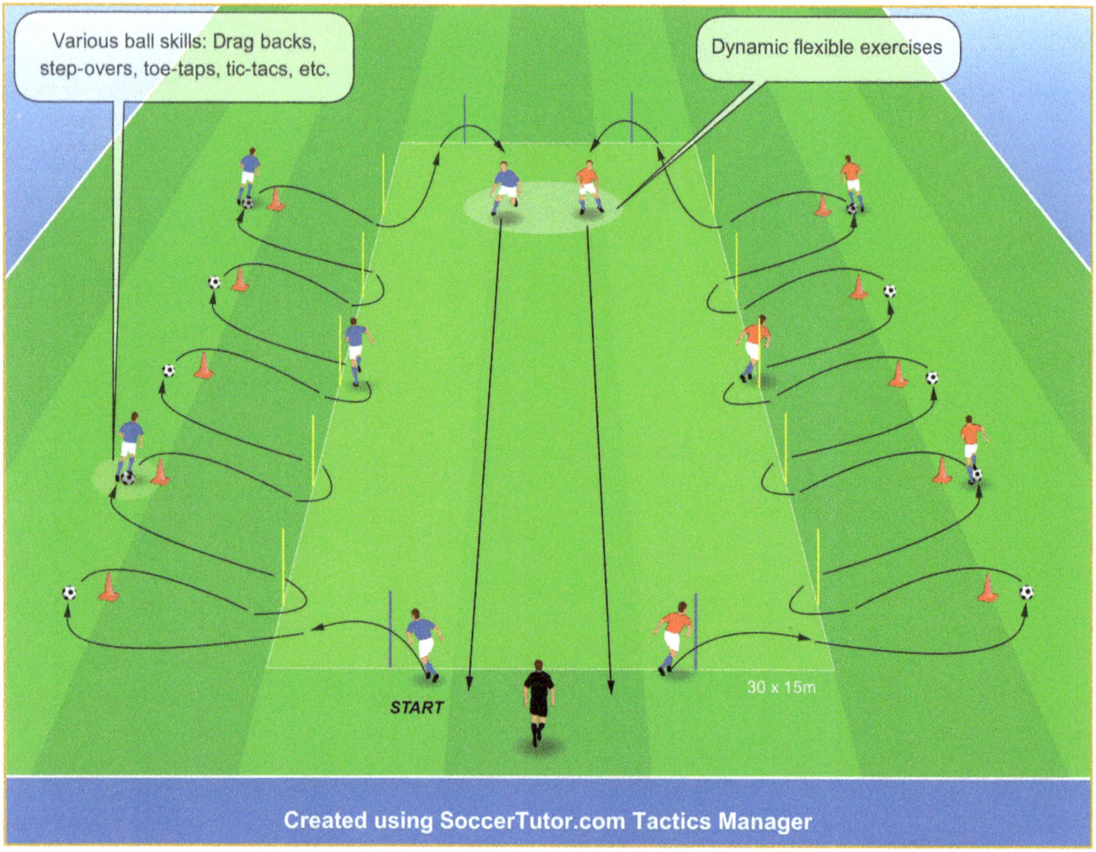

Duration	Reps	Sets	Numbers	Size (m)	Work Duration
8-10 min	1 Circuit	10	Groups of 5-10	30 Length	5-6 min

OBJECTIVE: Lateral speed, balance low to the ground, technique, and flexibility.

- In their 2 groups, the players run around the cones and poles in a zig-zag slalom pattern, as shown.

- Stationed at every red cone is a ball for the players to perform various ball skills, such as drag backs, step-over, toe-taps, tic-tacs, etc.

- After the final yellow pole, the players run around the end blue pole and back through the middle channel performing various dynamic flexibility movements, such as walking hamstring stretching, pre-turn, Russian walk, etc.

Resistance Warm Ups

Resistance 8. Coordination and Ball Control Skills Technical Warm Up Circuit

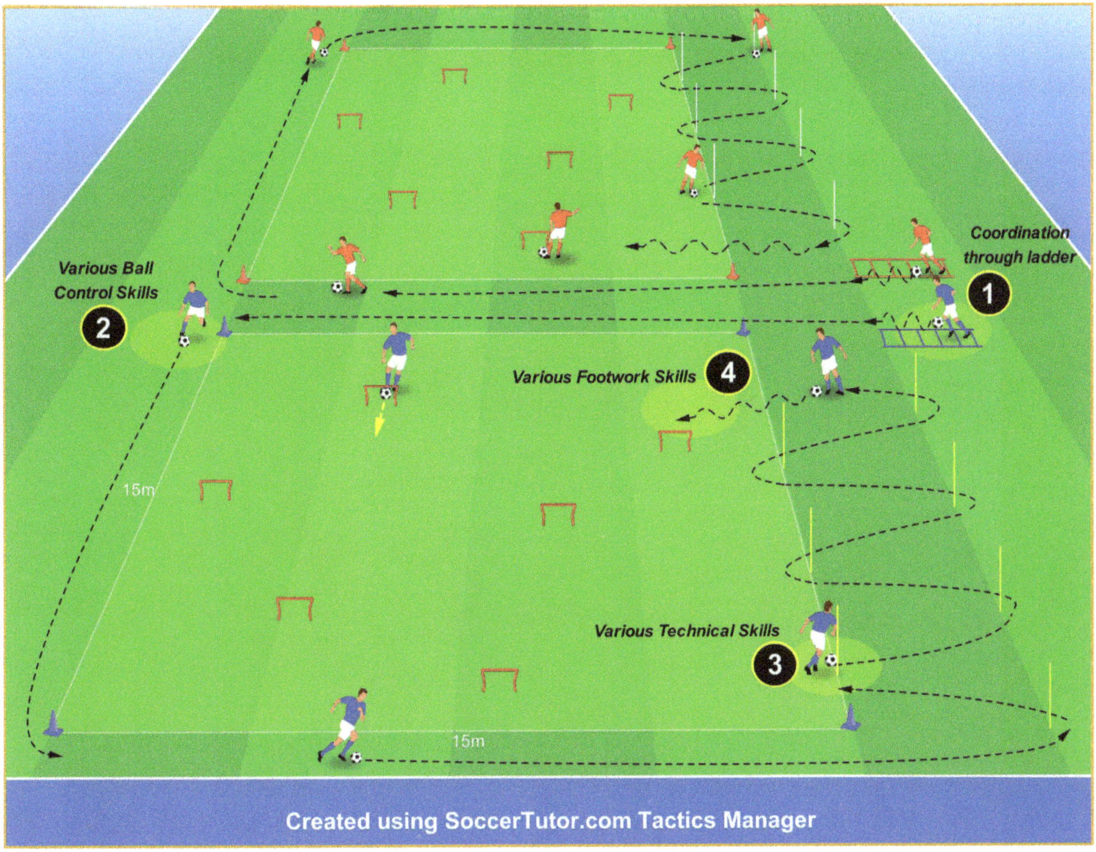

Duration	Reps	Sets	Numbers	Size (m)	Work Duration
15 min	3 min	3	2-20	15 x 15	9 min

OBJECTIVE: Balance, footwork, coordination, agility, strength, ball control, and speed.

Start with the players warming up without a ball, performing various dynamic flexibility exercises around the area. Progress to a warm up circuit with a ball.

1. Coordination work through ladder + dribble to cone.
2. Various ball control skills to cone.
3. Various technical skills to slalom through the poles.
4. Move into the centre to perform various footwork skills with the ball and low level plyometric and proprioception exercises with the hurdles.

Resistance Warm Ups

Resistance 9. "Brazilian Fast Feet" Dribbling and Ball Control + Agility Warm Up Circuit

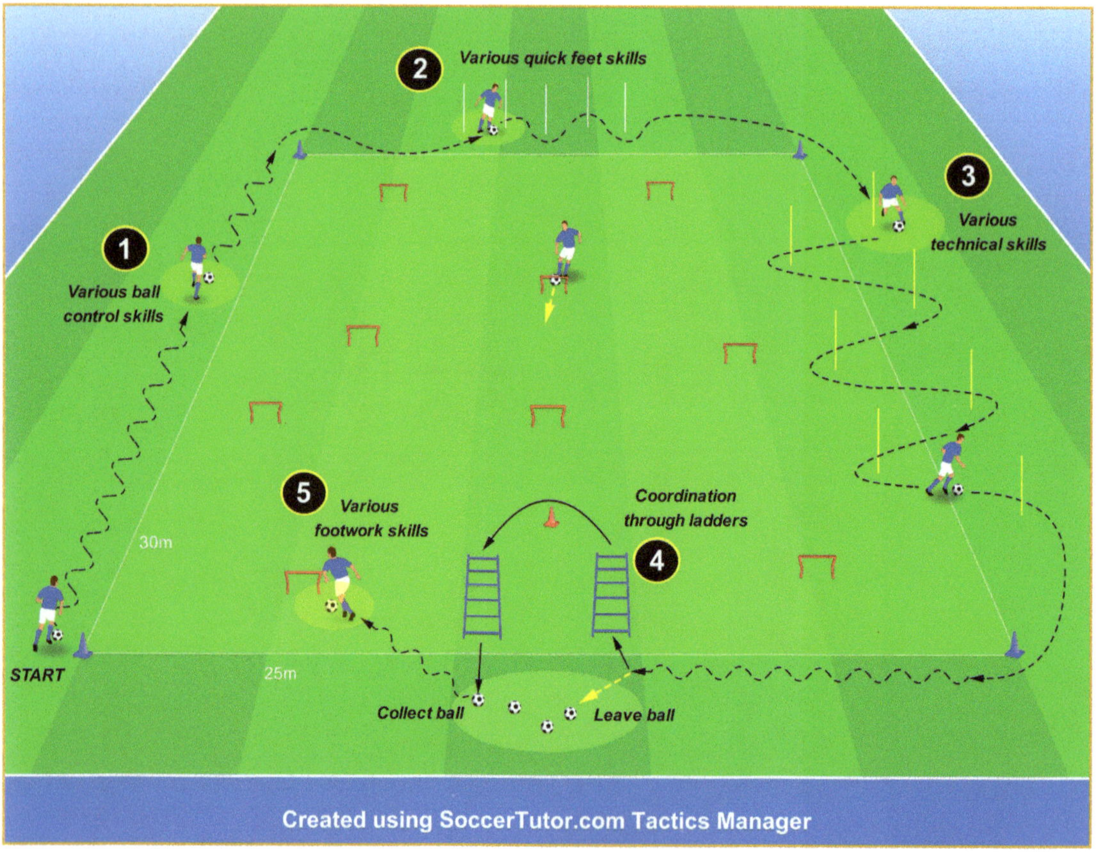

Duration	Reps	Sets	Numbers	Size (m)	Work Duration
15 min	3 min	3	2-10	30 x 25	9 min

OBJECTIVE: Balance, footwork, coordination, agility, strength, ball control, and speed.

- Players first warm up without a ball, performing dynamic flexibility exercises.
- They then start with a ball performing various ball control skills to the first cone, quick feet skills in between the 5 white poles, and various technical skills to slalom through the 7 yellow poles.
- They leave the ball and perform various coordination movements through both ladders, and then move back to the start.
- After collecting a ball again, the players perform various footwork skills and low level plyometric and proprioception exercises with the hurdles in the centre.

Resistance Warm Ups

Resistance 10. Ball Control, Agility, Speed, and Coordination Technical Warm Up Circuit

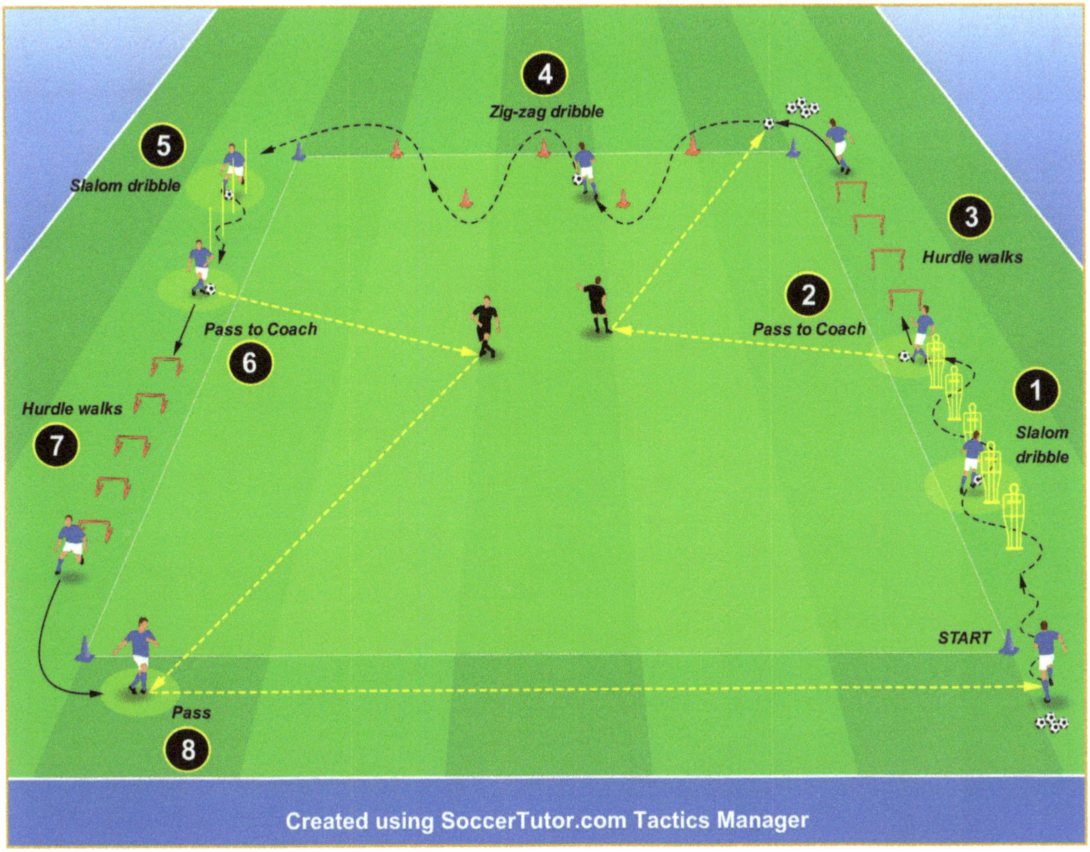

Duration	Reps	Sets	Numbers	Size (m)	Work Duration
15 min	2-3 min	3-5	8-20	30 x 20	10-15 min

OBJECTIVE: Agility, speed, coordination, ball control, and passing.

The players all work around the circuit, one behind the other with 2 coaches in the centre who act as support players.

1. Slalom dribble through the mannequins.
2. Pass to coach in the centre.
3. Walk through the hurdles.
4. Receive the coach's pass, then zig-zag dribble through the cones.
5. Slalom dribble through the poles.
6. Pass to the other coach in the centre.
7. Walk through the hurdles.
8. Receive coach's pass and pass to start.

Warm Ups to Maximise Performance

Resistance Warm Ups

Resistance 11. "Resistance V" Warm Up with Various Technical Skills in Pairs

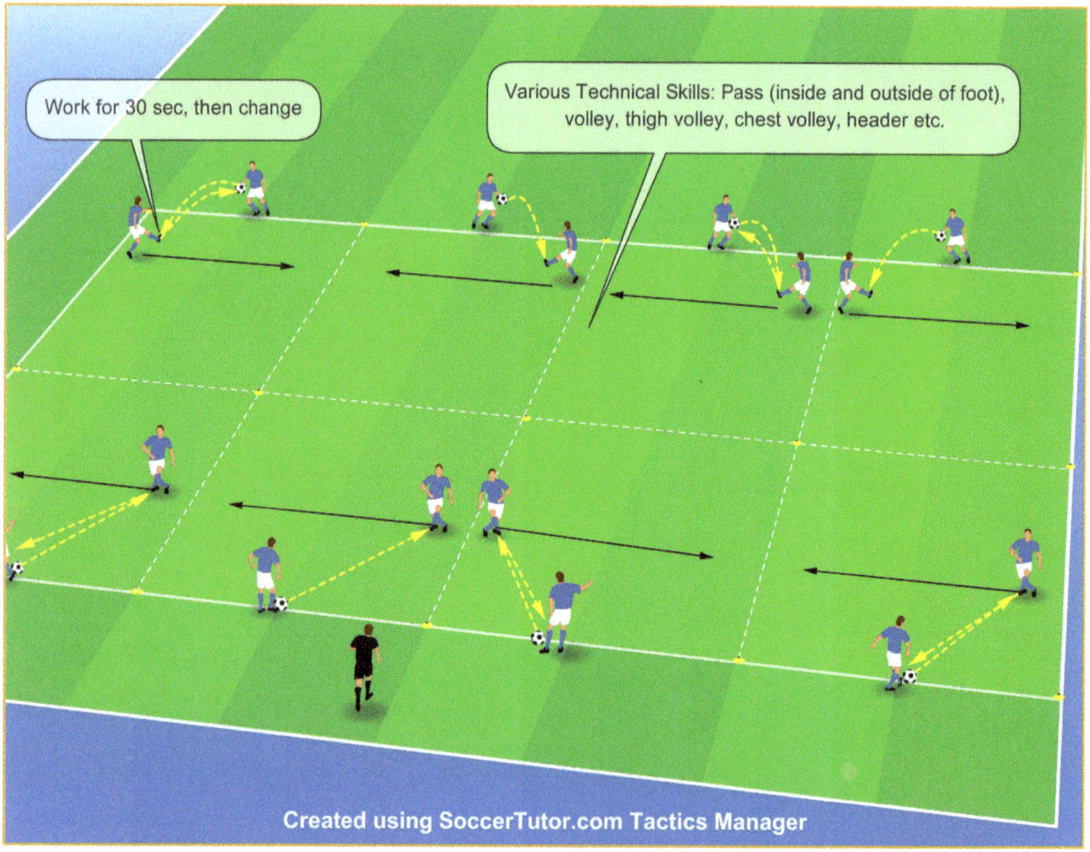

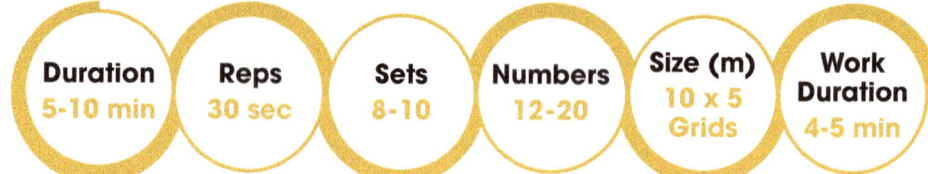

Duration	Reps	Sets	Numbers	Size (m)	Work Duration
5-10 min	30 sec	8-10	12-20	10 x 5 Grids	4-5 min

OBJECTIVE: Changes of direction, acceleration/deceleration, agility, and strength.

- In pairs, one player starts with the ball in hand, and the opposite player is shifting from left to right. The first player serves the ball (throws) and the other one performs volleys with both feet.

- The players change roles within their pairs every 30 seconds.

- Players perform various technical volley techniques: Volley, thigh volley, chest volley, header, inside and outside of foot volleys, etc.

- **VARIATION:** Forward and backward movement + headers back to the server (from server's throws).

Resistance Warm Ups

Resistance 12. One-Twos and "Switch" with Varied Movements Technical Warm Up

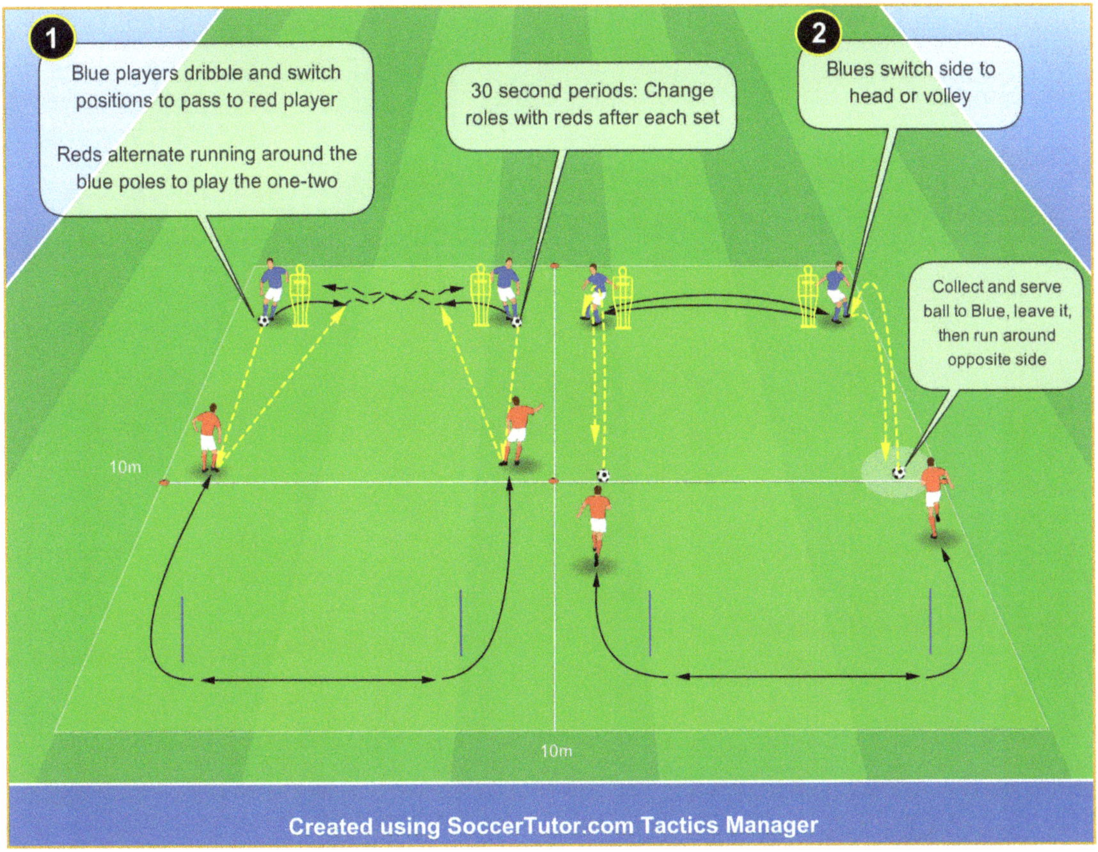

1 Blue players dribble and switch positions to pass to red player

Reds alternate running around the blue poles to play the one-two

30 second periods: Change roles with reds after each set

2 Blues switch side to head or volley

Collect and serve ball to Blue, leave it, then run around opposite side

Duration	Reps	Sets	Numbers	Size (m)	Work Duration
5-10 min	30 sec	10	Groups of 4	10 x 10	5 min

OBJECTIVE: Passing, receiving, dribbling, running with various different movements.

- Players are in groups of 4 and the 2 blue players start with a ball. **Blue 1** and **Blue 2** play a one-two (head, pass, or volley) with **Red 1** and **Red 2** respectively.

- **Blue 1** and **Blue 2** dribble their balls across to the other side to switch positions with each other.

- **Red 1** and **Red 2** run around the blue poles to switch positions.

- The coach can change the type of movements, rotating between forward, backward, and side-steps.

- **PROGRESSION:** Emphasis on gradually increasing the tempo of the movements.

Resistance Warm Ups

Resistance 13. Ball Control Skills "Nutmeg" Technical Warm Up in Pairs with Hurdle Gates

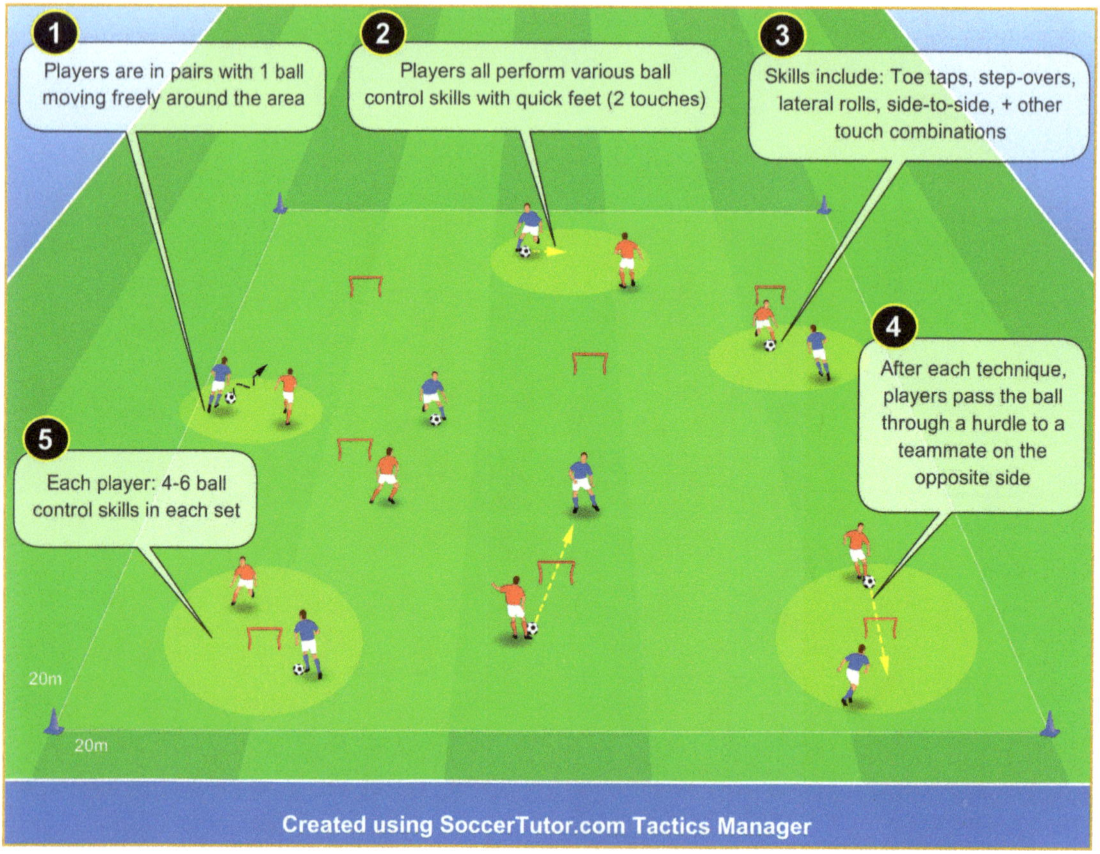

1. Players are in pairs with 1 ball moving freely around the area
2. Players all perform various ball control skills with quick feet (2 touches)
3. Skills include: Toe taps, step-overs, lateral rolls, side-to-side, + other touch combinations
4. After each technique, players pass the ball through a hurdle to a teammate on the opposite side
5. Each player: 4-6 ball control skills in each set

Duration	Reps	Sets	Numbers	Size (m)	Work Duration
5-10 min	3 min	3	2-20	20 x 20	9 min

OBJECTIVE: Quick feet, coordination, passing, and receiving.

- Players are in pairs with 1 ball and move freely around the area.
- The players all perform various ball control skills with quick feet (2 touches).
- Skills include toe taps forward and backward, step-overs, lateral rolls, side-to-side, and other touch combinations.
- After each technical execution, they pass the ball through a hurdle for their teammate to receive on the other side.
- Each player performs between 4-6 ball control skills in each set.

Resistance Warm Ups

Resistance 14. One-Two, Move to Receive, and Dynamic Flexibility "In & Out" Pairs Warm Up

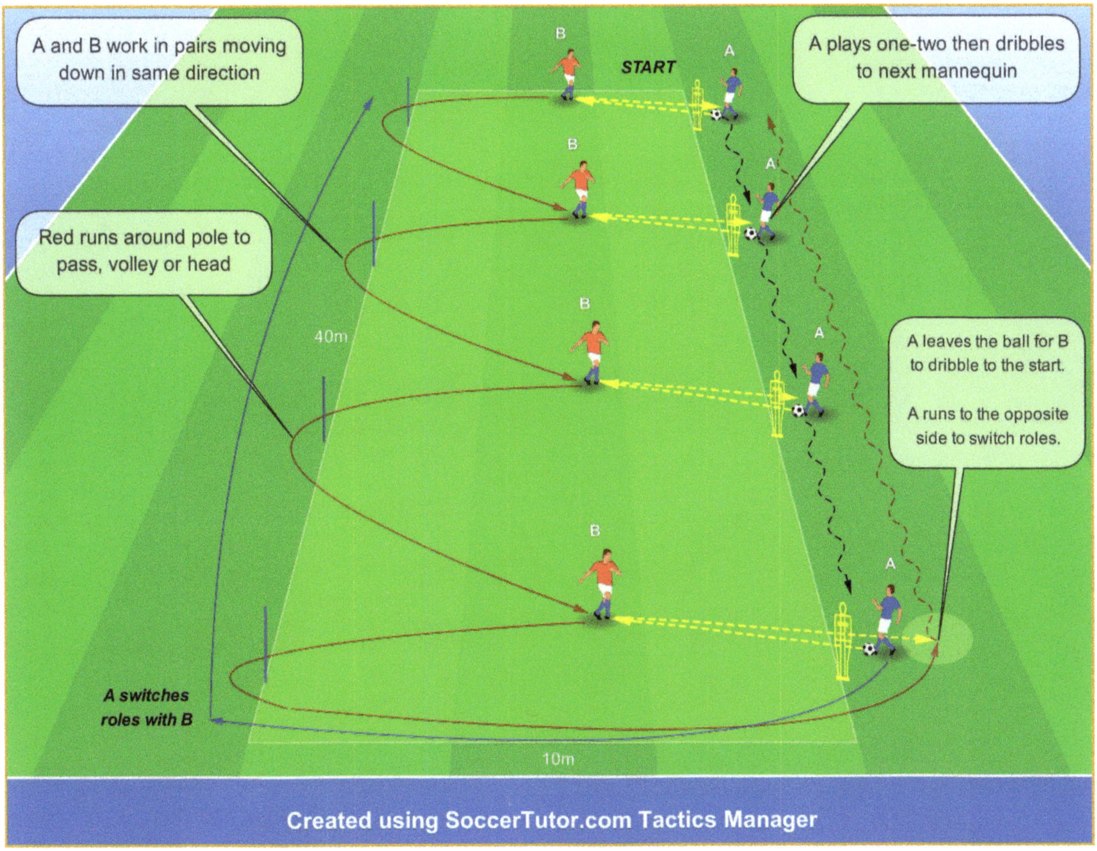

Diagram annotations:
- A and B work in pairs moving down in same direction
- A plays one-two then dribbles to next mannequin
- Red runs around pole to pass, volley or head
- A leaves the ball for B to dribble to the start. A runs to the opposite side to switch roles.
- A switches roles with B
- 40m / 10m / START

Created using SoccerTutor.com Tactics Manager

Duration	Reps	Sets	Numbers	Size (m)	Work Duration
5-10 min	1-3 min	3	8-10	40 x 10	5-10 min

OBJECTIVE: Passing, receiving, timing and speed of movements.

- Each of the pairs has a ball and the players all work in one direction
- **Player A** plays a one-two (head, pass, or volley) with **Player B**.
- **A** runs with the ball to the next position and **B** runs around the pole to prepare for the same sequence again.
- When they reach the end, the 2 players switch roles. **A** leaves the ball for **B** to dribble to the start and **B** performs various types of dynamic flexibility movements.
- This warm up can be developed into a high intensity aerobic practice.

53

©SOCCERTUTOR.COM   Warm Ups to Maximise Performance

Resistance Warm Ups

Resistance 15. Varied Movements and Dynamic Flexibility Zig-Zag Warm Up Circuit

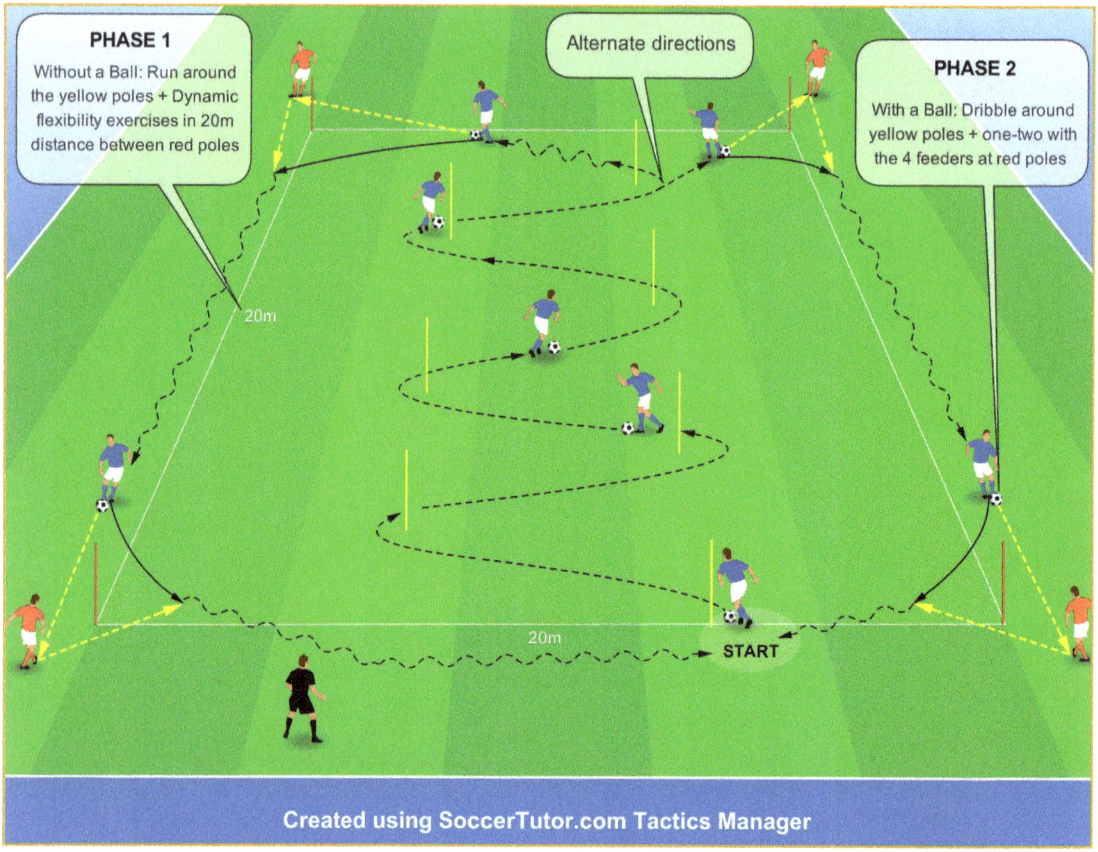

PHASE 1
Without a Ball: Run around the yellow poles + Dynamic flexibility exercises in 20m distance between red poles

Alternate directions

PHASE 2
With a Ball: Dribble around yellow poles + one-two with the 4 feeders at red poles

Duration	Reps	Sets	Numbers	Size (m)	Work Duration
10 min	2 min	3-4	10-12	20 x 20	6-8 min

OBJECTIVE: Basic warm up movements and dynamic flexibility exercises.

- **PHASE 1 (WITHOUT BALL):** The players run around the yellow poles in a zig-zag pattern using variations of movements: Forward, backward, side-steps, etc.
- Each player runs around the far left or right red pole (alternately) and performs dynamic flexibility exercises in the distance to the next red pole.

- **PHASE 2 (WITH BALL):** Players dribble around the yellow poles (zig-zag).
- Each player moves towards the left or right red pole (alternately) and plays a one-two with the red feeder player.
- They dribble to the next red pole, play another one-two, and move to the start.

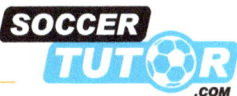

Resistance 16. Speed, Agility, and Coordination Technical "Give & Go" Warm Up Circuit

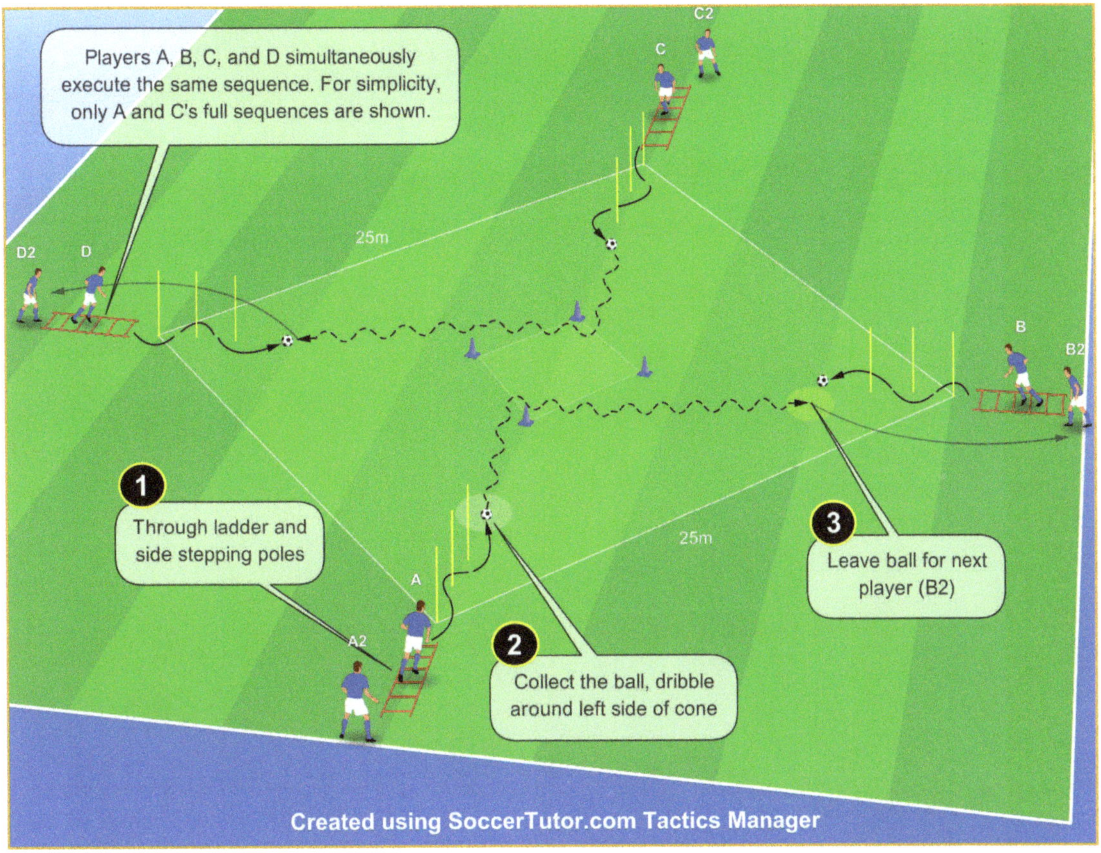

Players A, B, C, and D simultaneously execute the same sequence. For simplicity, only A and C's full sequences are shown.
C2
C
D2
D
25m
B
B2
1
Through ladder and side stepping poles
A
A2
2
Collect the ball, dribble around left side of cone
25m
3
Leave ball for next player (B2)
Created using SoccerTutor.com Tactics Manager

Duration	Reps	Sets	Numbers	Size (m)	Work Duration
10 min	4-5	3-4	8+	25 x 25	5-8 min

OBJECTIVE: Agility, coordination, and speed exercises with ball control.

- The players start from 4 different stations as shown using quick steps through the ladders, followed by side stepping through the poles.
- They collect the ball, dribble around the left side of the central cone, and then turn and dribble towards the right.
- Leaving the ball in front of the next set of poles, the player joins the next station.
- The coach changes the direction to clockwise after a set period of time.
- **PROGRESSION:** Create a speed endurance practice by adding specific work, rest ratios, and correct distances.

Resistance Warm Ups

Resistance 17. Speed, Agility, and Coordination Warm Up Circuit with Reactive "Tag Game"

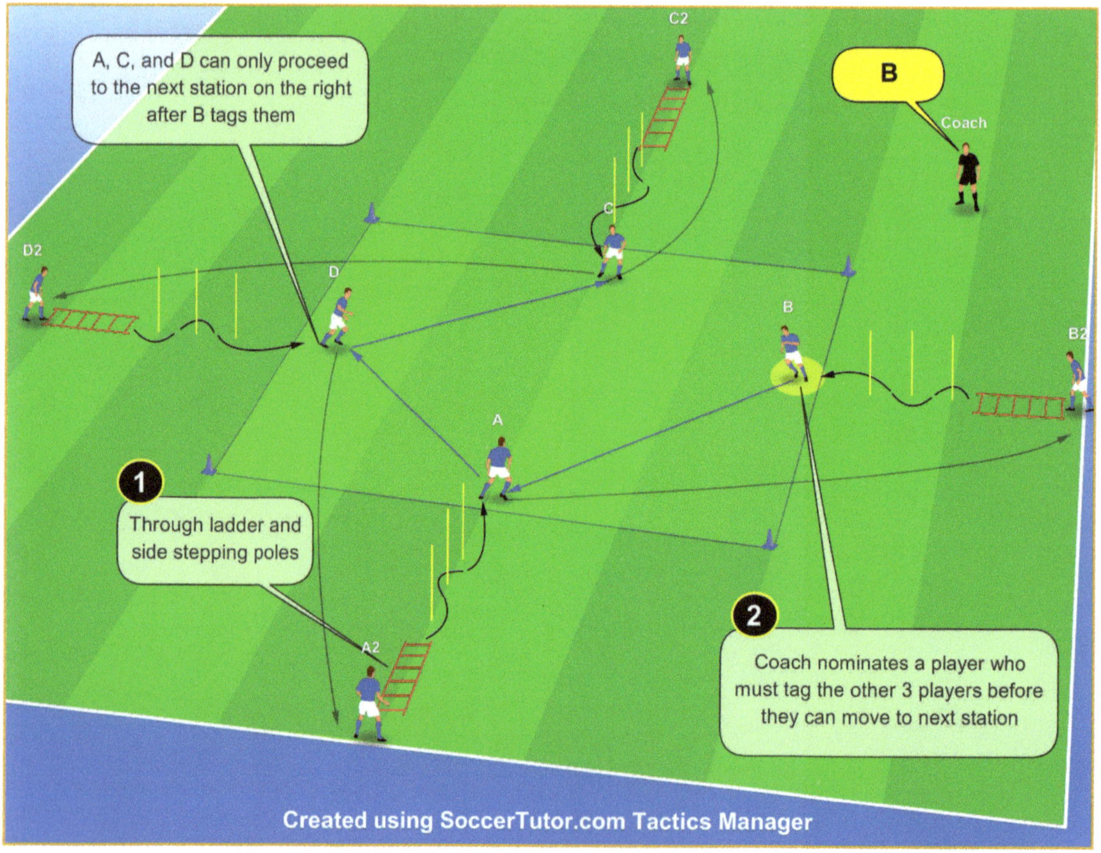

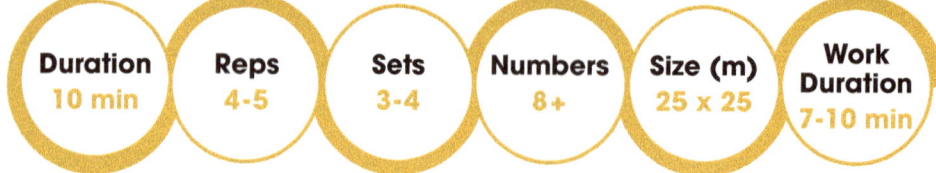

Duration	Reps	Sets	Numbers	Size (m)	Work Duration
10 min	4-5	3-4	8+	25 x 25	7-10 min

OBJECTIVE: Agility, coordination, and speed of movement (escaping markers).

- The players start from 4 different stations **(A, B, C, & D)** using quick steps through the ladders, side steps through the poles, and then move into the central area.

- One player is nominated as the "tagger." The aim is to tag each player before they can move to the next station and the next 4 waiting **(A2, B2, C2, & D2)** can go.

- **PROGRESSION:** Create a speed endurance practice by adding specific work, rest ratios, and correct distances.

Warm Ups to Maximise Performance

Resistance Warp Ups

Resistance 18. Speed, Agility, and Coordination Warm Up with Reactive "3v1 Possession"

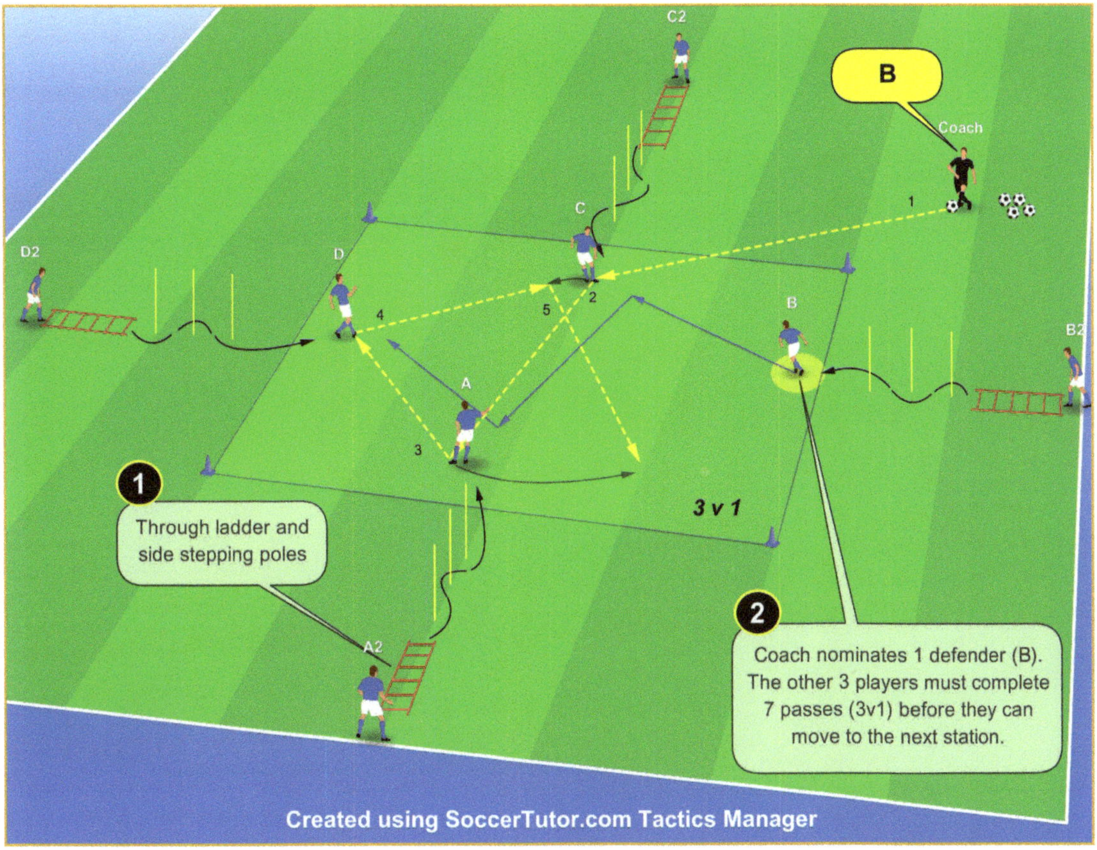

1 Through ladder and side stepping poles

2 Coach nominates 1 defender (B). The other 3 players must complete 7 passes (3v1) before they can move to the next station.

Duration	Reps	Sets	Numbers	Size (m)	Work Duration
10 min	4-5	3-4	8+	25 x 25	7-10 min

OBJECTIVE: Agility, coordination, and speed of movement (escaping markers).

- In this progression of the previous warm up, the players start from 4 different stations **(A, B, C, & D)** using quick steps through the ladders, side steps through the poles, and then move into the central area.

- The coach adds a ball into the central area and nominates 1 defender.

- The nominated defender in this example is **Player B**.

- The other 3 players must complete 7 passes in the central area vs **Player B** (defender) before they can move to the next station and the next 4 players waiting **(A2, B2, C2, & D2)** can go.

Warm Ups to Maximise Performance

Resistance Warm Ups

Resistance 19. "Crossfire" Passing, Agility, and Speed 4-Corners Technical Warm Up

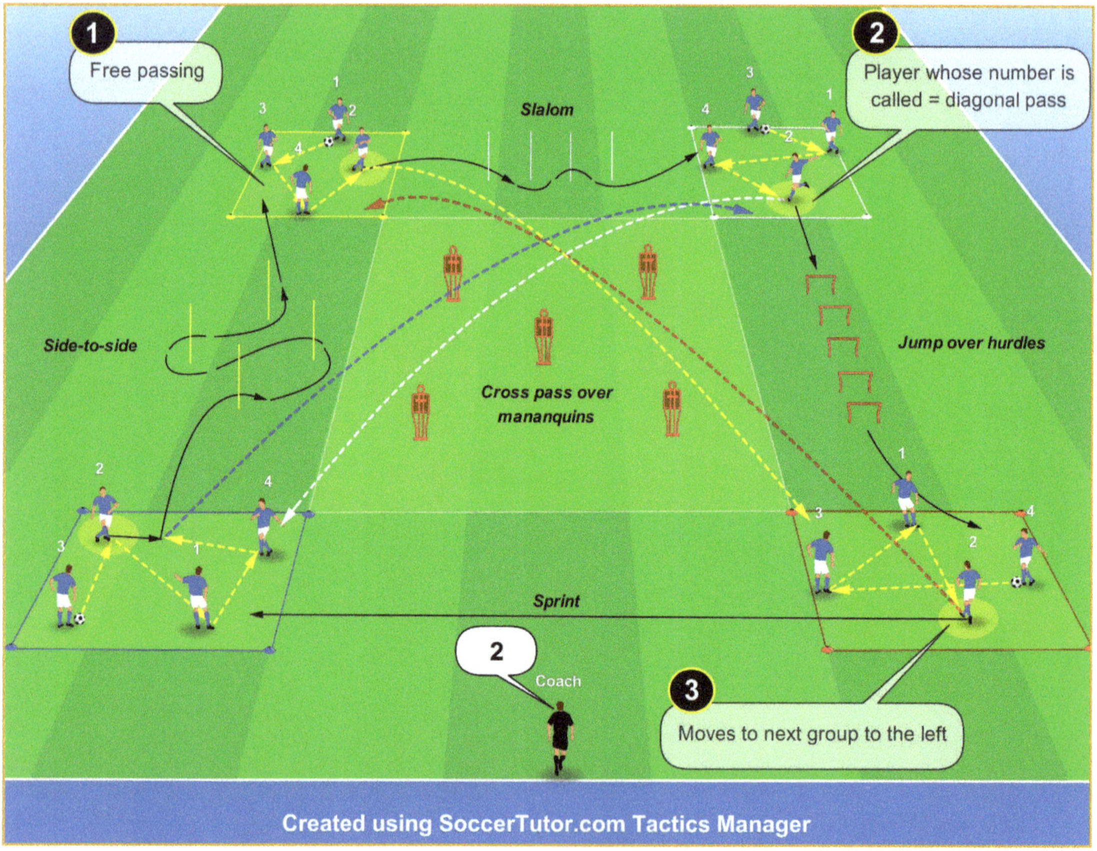

Duration	Reps	Sets	Numbers	Size (m)	Work Duration
10-15 min	2-3 min	3-5	16-20	40 x 30	10-12 min

OBJECTIVE: Passing (short and long), receiving, coordination, agility, and speed.

- Players are in groups of 4 or 5 in the corner areas and start by passing freely to each other.

- When the coach calls out a number (1-4), that player (**Player 2** in diagram example) in all 4 corners plays a diagonal pass to the opposite group, making sure to avoid the mannequins.

- **Player 2** must then move to the group to their left, performing either a sprint, side-to-side through poles, slalom through poles, or jump over small hurdles along the way.

- We continue with free passing, waiting for the coach to call out a new number.

Resistance Warm Ups

Resistance 20. Attack vs Defence Warm Up with Passive Jockeying Movements

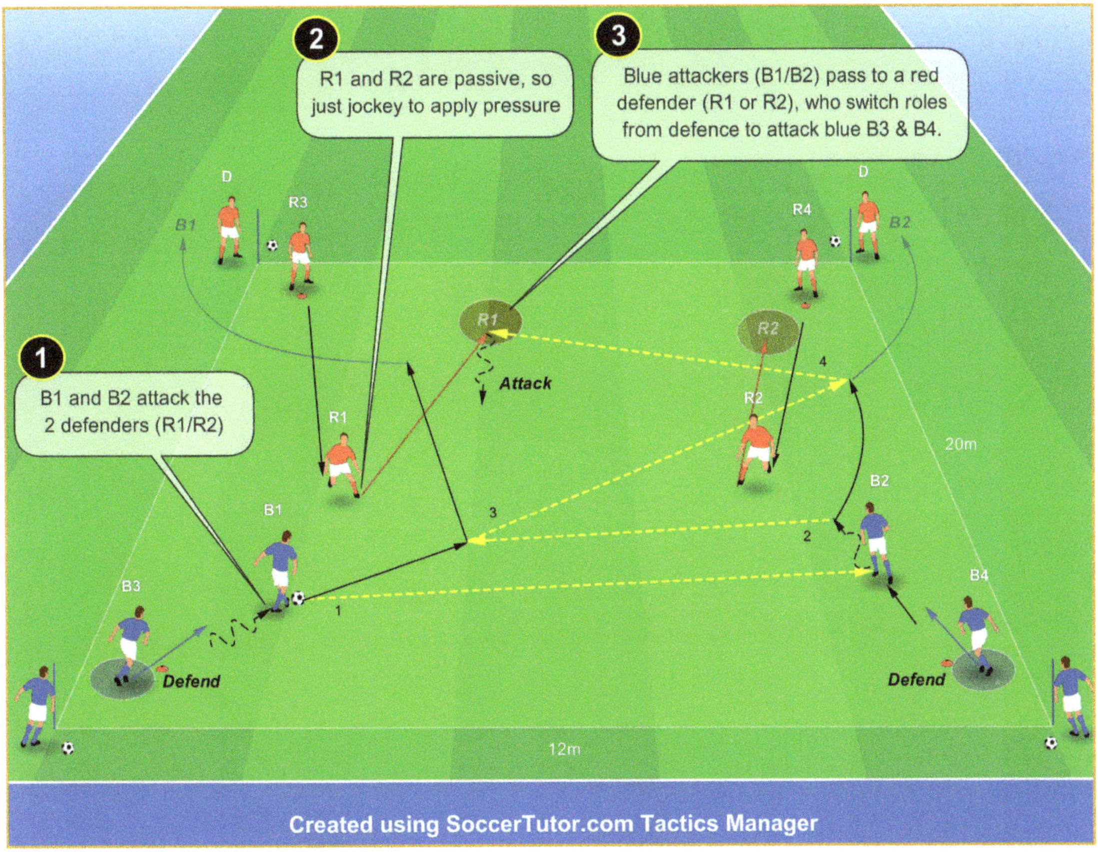

1. B1 and B2 attack the 2 defenders (R1/R2)

2. R1 and R2 are passive, so just jockey to apply pressure

3. Blue attackers (B1/B2) pass to a red defender (R1 or R2), who switch roles from defence to attack blue B3 & B4.

Duration	Reps	Sets	Numbers	Size (m)	Work Duration
15 min	3 min	3-5	12-20	20 x 12	5-6 min

OBJECTIVE: Changes of direction, agility, defensive movements, and coordination.

- Start by playing 2v2 passively, so the defenders just jockey to apply pressure.
- The practice starts with 2 pairs (reds vs blues) and **B1** passes to **B2**. They then attack the 2 red defenders (R1 and R2).
- **R1** and **R2** perform backward jockeying movements.
- **B2** passes the ball to **R1**, and the red pair now move forward to attack the next 2 blue players, who move forward (**B3** and **B4** = new defenders).
- Each pair's sequence is 1) Defend in 2v2 situation → 2) Attack in 2v2 situation → 3) Move out of the area.

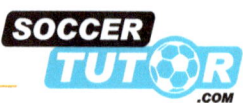

Resistance 21. Collective Team Pressing in Relation to Ball Position "Sacchi" Warm Up

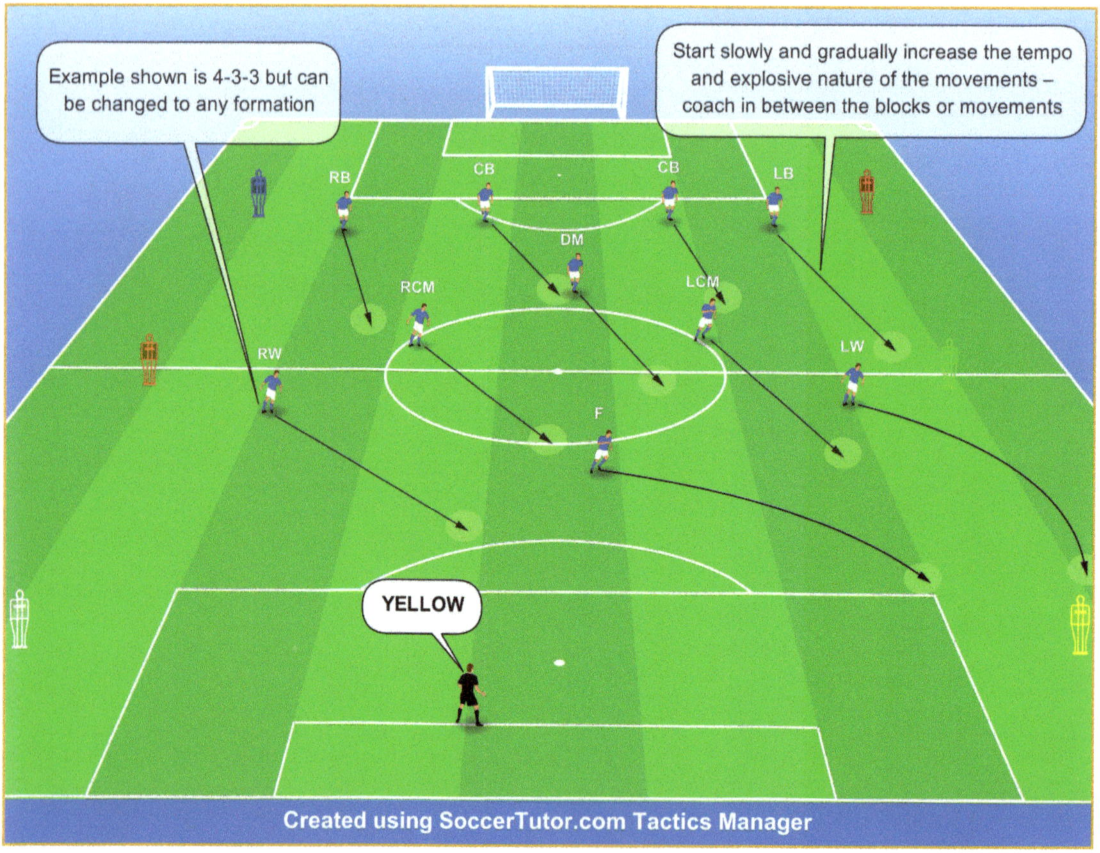
Example shown is 4-3-3 but can be changed to any formation
Start slowly and gradually increase the tempo and explosive nature of the movements – coach in between the blocks or movements
RB
CB
CB
LB
DM
RCM
LCM
RW
LW
F
YELLOW
Created using SoccerTutor.com Tactics Manager

Duration	Reps	Sets	Numbers	Size (m)	Work Duration
20 min	1 min	5	10	Full Pitch	5 min

OBJECTIVE: Pressing, collective movement, compactness, and speed endurance.

- The example shows the 4-3-3 formation, but you can use any formation.
- There are 6 different coloured mannequins (or cones). When a colour is called out by the coach, the players then move together to press that mannequin as though it was an opposition player in possession of the ball.
- On the coach's whistle, the players return to their starting position to wait for the next colour to be called.
- The players perform 5 x 1 minute sets and work at 70-80% of their maximum heart rate. Allow a full 3 minutes rest after each set for the players to recover.

Speed Endurance Warm Ups

SPEED ENDURANCE WARM UPS

Speed Endurance Warm Up Practices

The principles in *"Football Periodization" (see pages 10-11 for details)* underscore the importance of the *Speed Endurance Warm Up*, aligning it with the upcoming coaching content. Tailored for sessions featuring **long accelerations**, **extensive high speed running**, and **sprint related activities**, these warm ups involve repetitive football movements at higher speeds, which prepare players for the specific demands of such actions.

Strategic Implementation

Larger Based Density & High Speed Running Training Preparation

Incorporating speed endurance warm ups is crucial, especially on **training days with extended accelerations and significant high speed running** and sprinting. The **expansive pitch dimensions require sustained near maximal speed**, demanding physiological and biomechanical readiness (Djaoui et al., 2017; Malone et al., 2018).

The speed endurance warm up serves as a carefully planned preparation, making sure the **players are fully prepared for the heightened physical challenges in the main training session** on such days.

Impact on Muscle Groups

1. Hamstring Muscles

- Speed endurance warm ups target hamstrings, which are vital for prolonged accelerations and sprints.
- Repetitive high speed demands prompt muscle adaptation, reducing injury risk.
- Essential to initiate warm ups specific to upcoming sessions.

2. Calf Muscles

- Crucial for rapid accelerations, calves are a focus in speed endurance warm ups.
- These warm ups prepare muscles for explosive speed work on training days.
- Gradual engagement enhances neuromuscular activation, optimising functionality and potentially reducing fatigue issues with consistent load management.

Muscular Adaptation to Training Stimulus

Tailored for sustained high speed distances and sprints, the speed endurance warm ups deliberately challenge muscles at a gradual level, stimulating resilience and adaptability.

According to Malone et al. (2018), exposing players to rapid increases in high speed running during training may increase the likelihood of injury, but higher chronic training loads and better aerobic fitness offset this risk.

Summary

Speed Endurance Warm Ups strategically ready players for:

1. Sustained accelerations and high speed actions.
2. Minimising injury risk.
3. Optimising performance.
4. Preparing for upcoming training sessions.

Speed Endurance Warm Ups

3 DAYS UNTIL MATCH (MD +4/-3)

Collective Team Principle Training and Speed Endurance

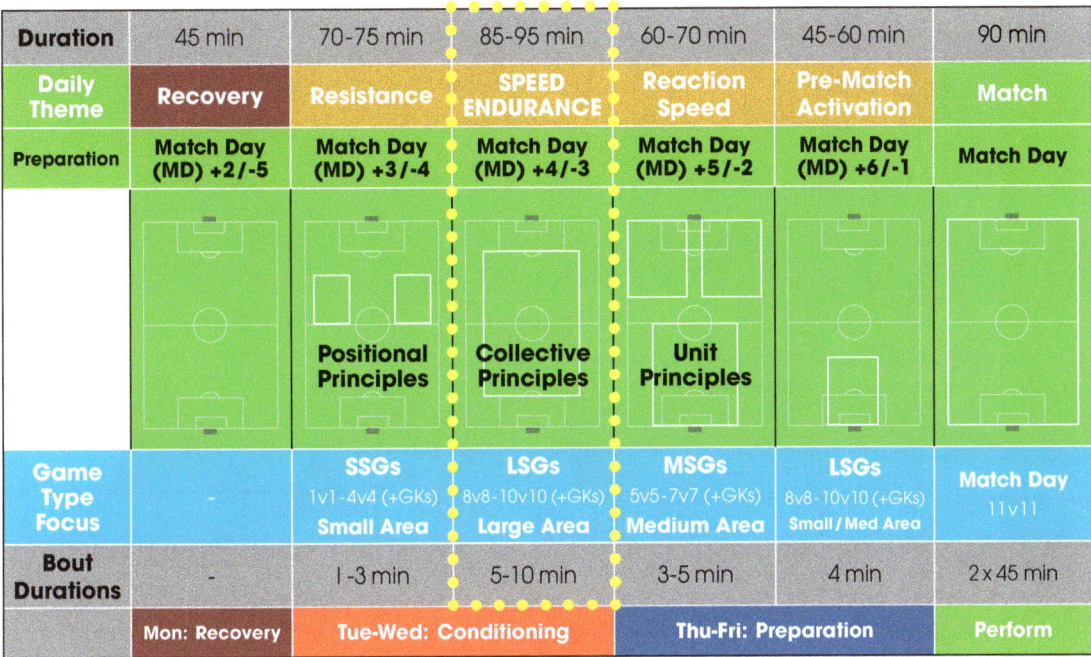

Duration	45 min	70-75 min	85-95 min	60-70 min	45-60 min	90 min
Daily Theme	Recovery	Resistance	**SPEED ENDURANCE**	Reaction Speed	Pre-Match Activation	Match
Preparation	Match Day (MD) +2/-5	Match Day (MD) +3/-4	Match Day (MD) +4/-3	Match Day (MD) +5/-2	Match Day (MD) +6/-1	Match Day
		Positional Principles	Collective Principles	Unit Principles		
Game Type Focus	-	SSGs 1v1-4v4 (+GKs) Small Area	LSGs 8v8-10v10 (+GKs) Large Area	MSGs 5v5-7v7 (+GKs) Medium Area	LSGs 8v8-10v10 (+GKs) Small/Med Area	Match Day 11v11
Bout Durations	-	1-3 min	5-10 min	3-5 min	4 min	2 x 45 min
	Mon: Recovery	Tue-Wed: Conditioning		Thu-Fri: Preparation		Perform

* **Training Week based on Professional Microcycle Example** - see pages 20-21.

Key Focus on:

- **Collective Principles and Game Principles** at near maximum speed
- **Speed Endurance**
- **Physical Overloads** within larger training areas per player (density) and positional/tactical structure

Speed Endurance Warm Ups

SPEED ENDURANCE TRAINING SESSION
3 Days Until Match (MD +4/-3)

Collective Team Principle Training and Speed Endurance (85-95 min):

1. Speed Endurance Warm Up (10-12 min)
2. Extensive Technical Practice (12-15 min)
3. Speed Endurance Conditioning Practice (5-15 min)
4. Large Sided Possession (10-15 min)
5. Large Sided Game in Large Area (10-50 min)

Speed Endurance Warm Ups

3 DAYS UNTIL MATCH (MD +4/-3)
Speed Endurance Warm Up Practices

INTENSITY: All practices are performed at full intensity

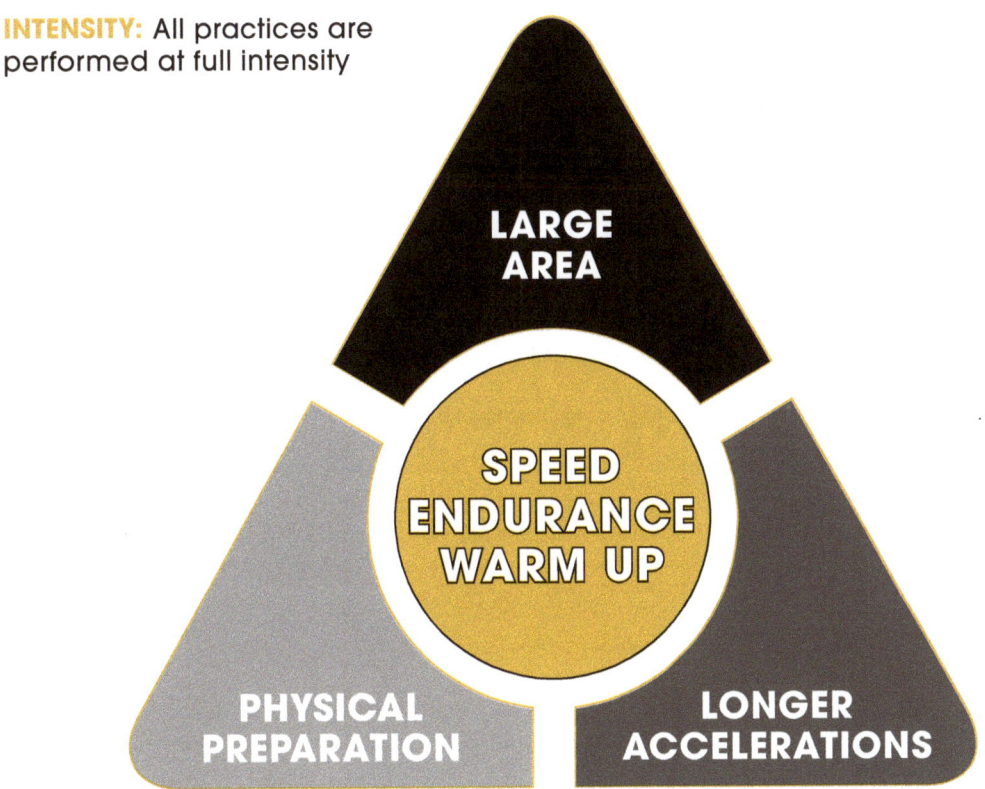

What are Speed Endurance Warm Ups?

- Speed endurance warm ups are inclusive of less aggressive or explosive directional changes but include more longer acceleration based work in more expansive (larger) spaces.

- The bigger surface area provides the opportunity to engage the hamstrings through more high-speed running exposures.

Why are they used on this day of the training week (MD +4/-3)?

- To prepare the players for the larger surface area type work developed through the course of the session.

How does this help to maximise performance?

- To best prepare the players' muscles for larger, high speed sprint based efforts.

- Generally readying the body for the session ahead (large sided games).

Speed Endurance Warm Ups

Hamstring Activity at Different Running Speeds

Reference: Hegyi etal. MSSE 2019   Designed by @YLMSportScience

Hamstring muscle activation was evaluated in 13 team sport athletes on a treadmill at 3 steady speeds:

14.8 km/h (slow)

19.4 km/h (moderate)

24.5 km/h (fast)

WHAT THEY FOUND

1. Hamstring muscle activation appears to be entirely individual.
2. Sprinting maximally in training is key to reducing hamstring strains + running at various speeds in rehabilitation is fundamental (with gradual exposure over time).

 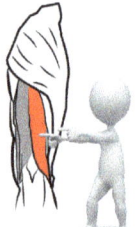  

BUT these individual patterns are consistent through the 3 speeds assessed here.

PRACTICAL APPLICATIONS

1. If everyone has their own pattern of hamstring activation, the only way to recreate this pattern is by running.
2. It may be crucial to implement running at submaximal speeds early after hamstring injury, instead of focusing exclusively on gym-based loading.
3. Maximal velocity running must be part of a well-rounded hamstring injury prevention program since it is associated with a much greater level of muscle activation than any gym-based exercise.

©SOCCERTUTOR.COM   Warm Ups to Maximise Performance

Speed Endurance Warm Ups

Speed Endurance 1. Dynamic Flexibility and Agility "Fast Feet" Warm Up Circuit

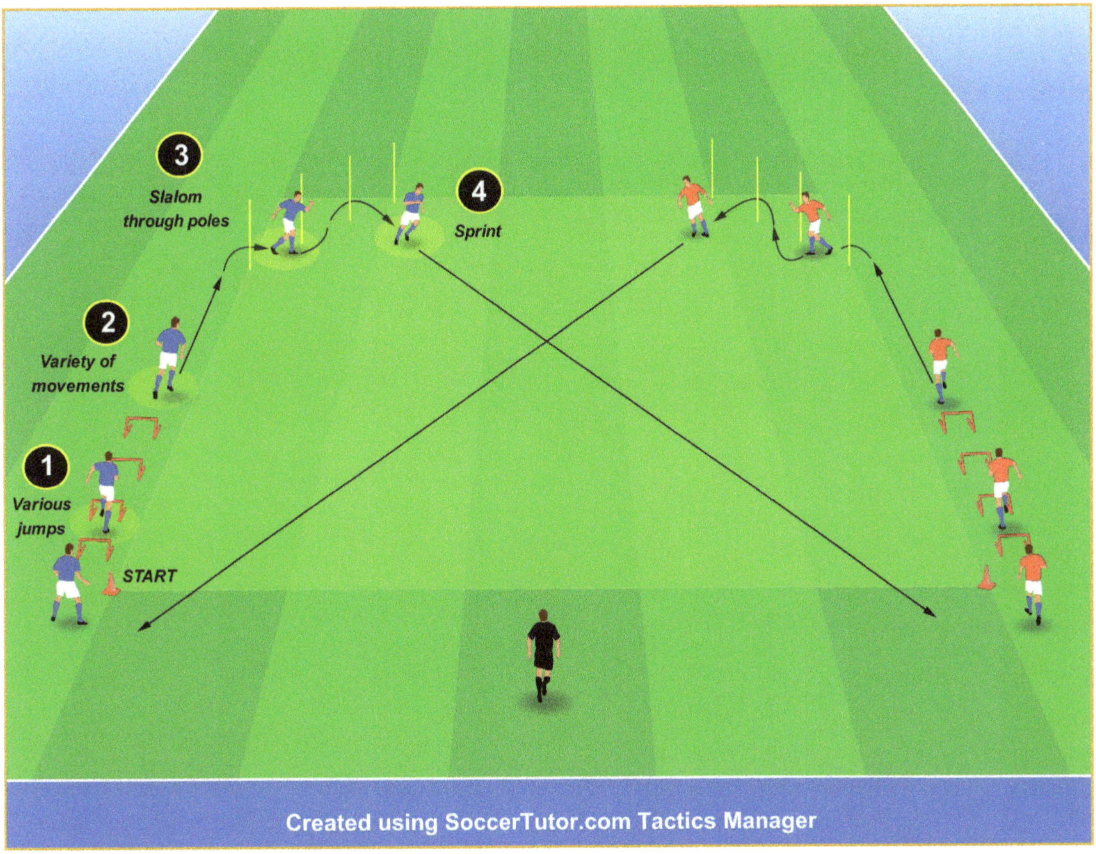

Duration	Reps	Sets	Numbers	Size (m)	Work Duration
10 min	4 x Circuit	3-5	4-20	30 x 20	5-6 min

OBJECTIVE: Dynamic flexibility, agility, explosive power, and speed.

The players move around the circuit in a figure of 8 shape:

1. Different types of jumps over 4 hurdles determined by the coach.
2. Variety of movements e.g. backward, side-steps, high knees, etc.
3. Slalom running through the poles.
4. Diagonal sprint to join the opposite side (the 2 players cross over).

→ Gradually increase the intensity of work and speed from 70% to 90% effort.

PROGRESSION: Introduce balls so the players dribble around the circuit instead.

Speed Endurance Warm Ups

Speed Endurance 2. Coordination and Fast Footwork "Crossover" Warm Up Circuit

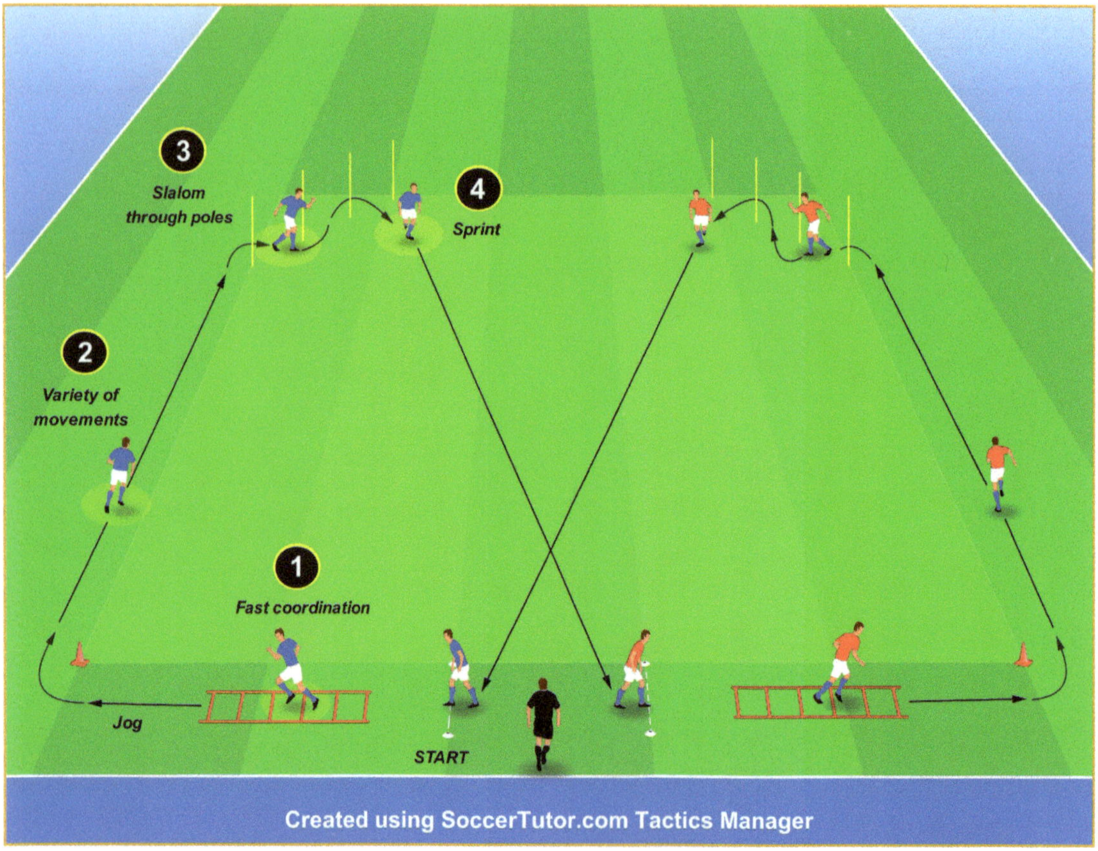

Duration	Reps	Sets	Numbers	Size (m)	Work Duration
10 min	4 x Circuit	3-5	4-20	30 x 20	5-6 min

OBJECTIVE: Dynamic flexibility, coordination, explosive power, and speed.

The players move around the circuit in a figure of 8 shape:

1. Fast steps through the ladders with quick feet and run around the cone.
2. Move between the cone and poles performing a variety of movements e.g. backwards, side-steps, high knees, etc.
3. Slalom running through the poles.
4. Diagonal sprint to join the opposite side (the 2 players cross over).

→ Gradually increase the intensity of work and speed from 70% to 90% effort.

PROGRESSION: Intensity can be increased by adding a time limit to complete circuit.

Speed Endurance Warm Ups

Speed Endurance 3. Coordination, Agility, and Flexibility Varied Tempo Warm Up Circuit

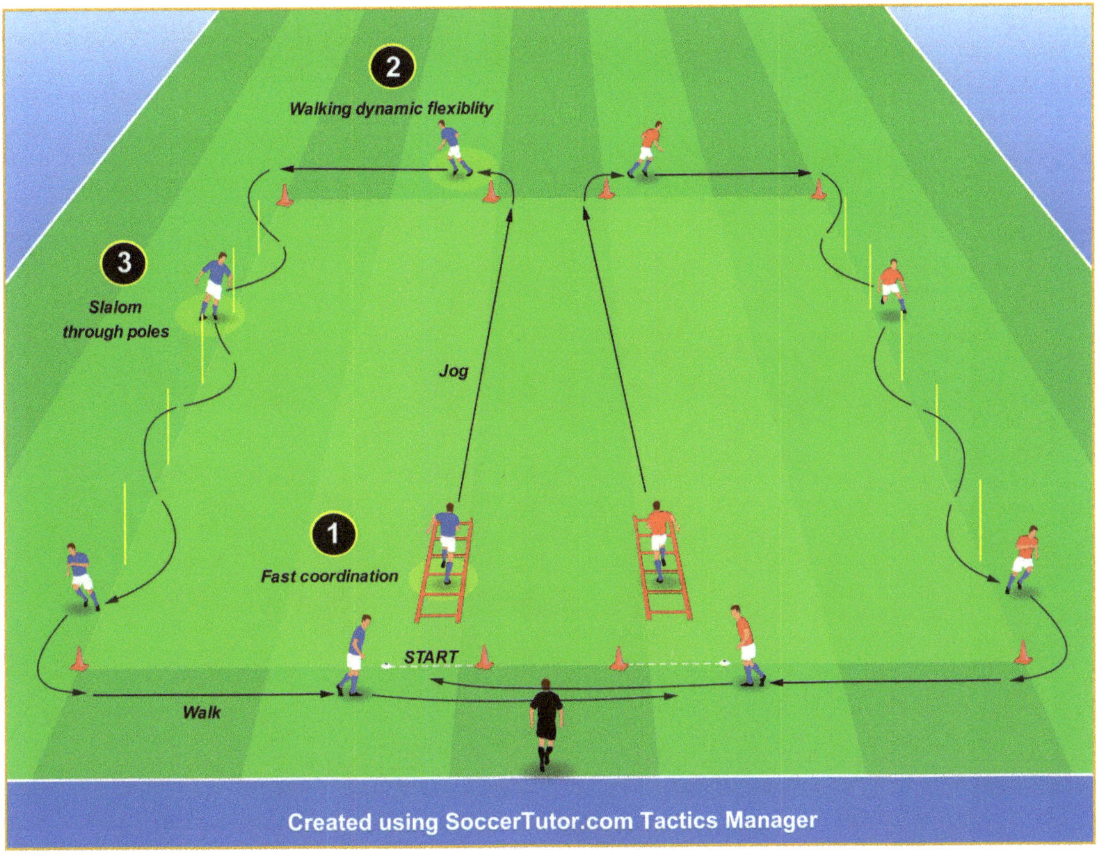

Duration	Reps	Sets	Numbers	Size (m)	Work Duration
10 min	2 min	3-4	4-20	25 Length	6-8 min

OBJECTIVE: Speed, coordination, balance, and dynamic flexibility training.

This continuous circuit warm up practice focuses on dynamic flexibility while varying the tempo throughout. The players start with some static stretching exercises, then:

1. Move fast through the ladders with quick feet and jog around the cone.
2. Walk through various dynamic flexibility exercises e.g. walking hamstring stretching, pre-turn, Russian walk, from the cone to the poles.
3. Slalom running through the poles and walk back to the start.

→ Gradually increase the intensity of work.

Speed Endurance Warm Ups

Speed Endurance 4. Coordination, Balance, and Flexibility Varied Tempo Warm Up Circuit

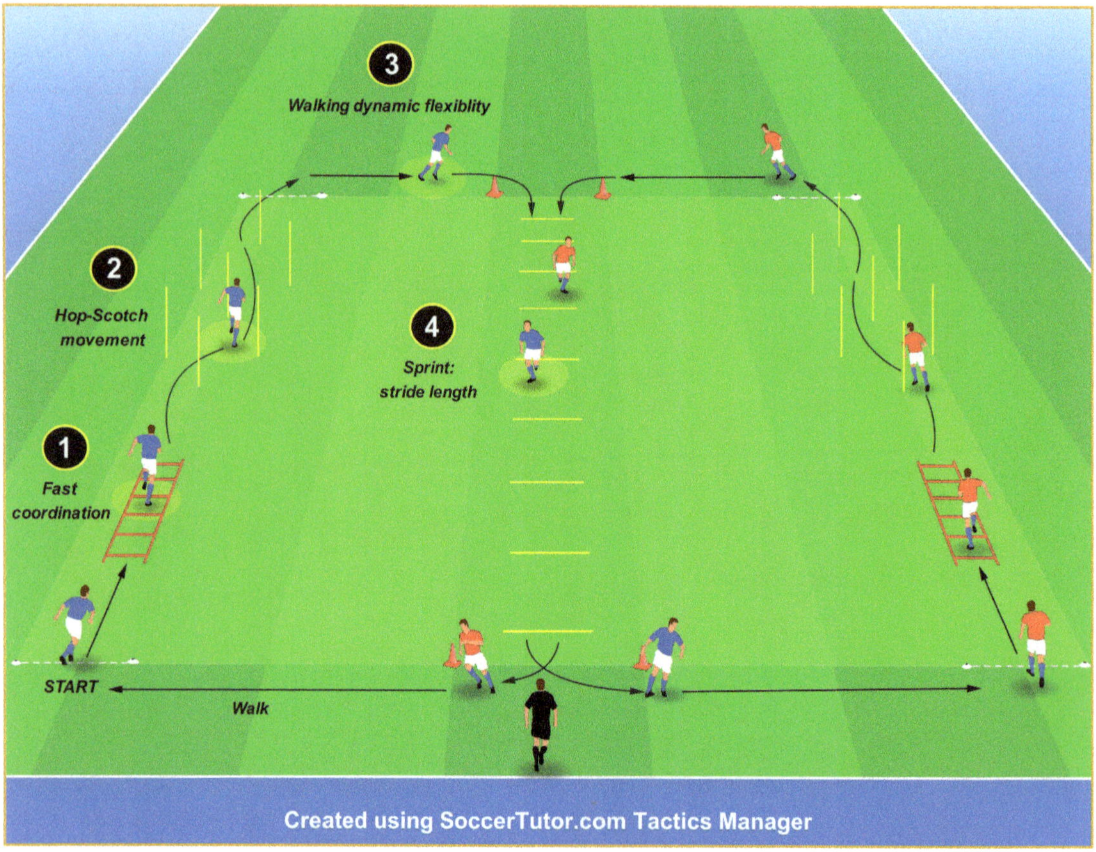

Duration	Reps	Sets	Numbers	Size (m)	Work Duration
10 min	1-2 min	3-5	4-20	25 Length	6-8 min

OBJECTIVE: Speed, coordination, balance, and dynamic flexibility training.

This continuous 2-sided circuit warm up practice focuses on dynamic flexibility while varying the tempo throughout:

1. Move fast through the ladders with quick feet, performing various coordination movements.
2. "Hop-Scotch" movement through poles.
3. Walking dynamic flexibility exercises e.g. walking hamstring stretching, pre-turn, Russian walk, etc. Then walk through the cone gate.
4. Sprint through the stride length markers (distances increase) and walk to the back of the other group.

Speed Endurance Warm Ups

Speed Endurance 5. Dynamic Mobility, Agility, and Power Warm Up Circuit

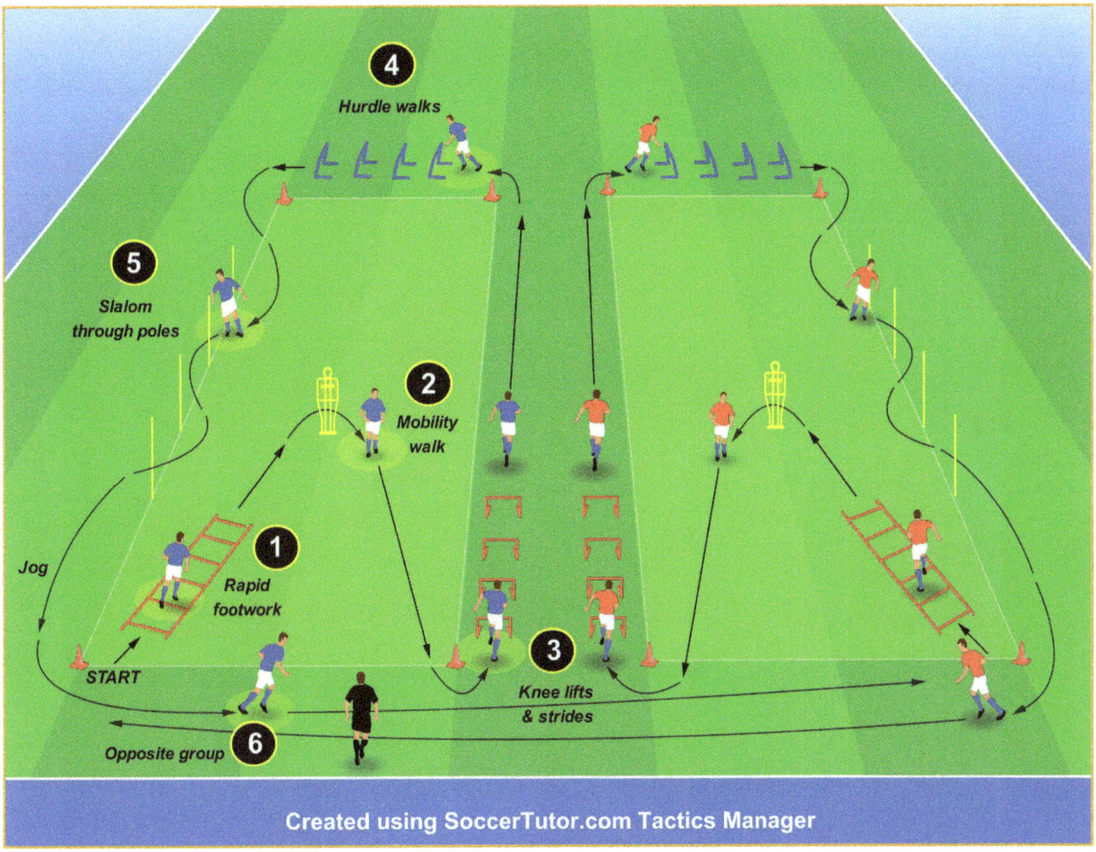

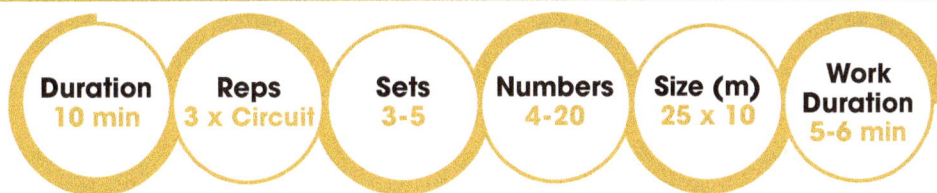

Duration	Reps	Sets	Numbers	Size (m)	Work Duration
10 min	3 x Circuit	3-5	4-20	25 x 10	5-6 min

OBJECTIVE: Physical muscle mobility work with speed endurance training.

1. Starting in the bottom left corner, the players perform rapid footwork through the ladder.
2. Walk using mobility exercises around the mannequin to the cone.
3. Knee lifts and strides through 4 hurdles + sprint to cone.
4. Hurdle walks (mobility) over 4 hurdles.
5. Slalom run through the poles and jog to the start position.
6. Continue with the continuous circuit.
→ Gradually increase intensity of work and speed from 70% to 90% effort.

Speed Endurance Warm Ups

Speed Endurance 6. Mobility, Coordination, and Sprinting Triangle Warm Up Circuit

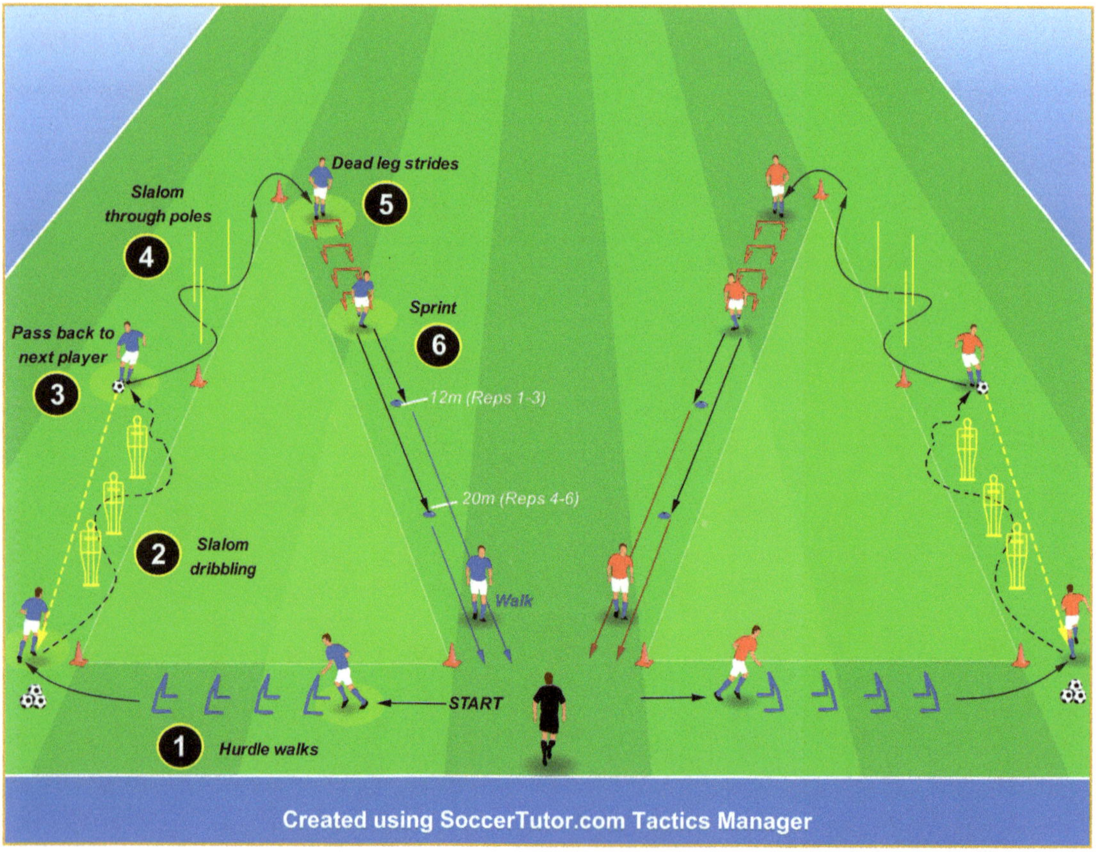

Duration	Reps	Sets	Numbers	Size (m)	Work Duration
10 min	3 x Circuit	3-5	4-20	25 x 10	5-6 min

OBJECTIVE: Physical muscle mobility work, explosive power, and speed endurance.

1. Hurdle walks (mobility) over 4 hurdles.
2. Collect ball and perform slalom dribbling through the mannequins up to the cone.
3. Pass ball back to next player behind.
4. Slalom running through the poles and around the cone at point of triangle.
5. "Dead-leg" strides through 4 hurdles.
6. For reps 1 to 3, the players sprint 12m to the first cone, then walk to the start. For reps 4 to 6, they sprint 20m to the second cone, then walk to the start. For reps 7 to 9, they sprint 25m to the start.

→ Gradually increase the intensity of work and speed from 70% to 90% effort.

Speed Endurance Warm Ups

Speed Endurance 7. Technical Stop, Start, Pass, and Running With the Ball Circuit Training

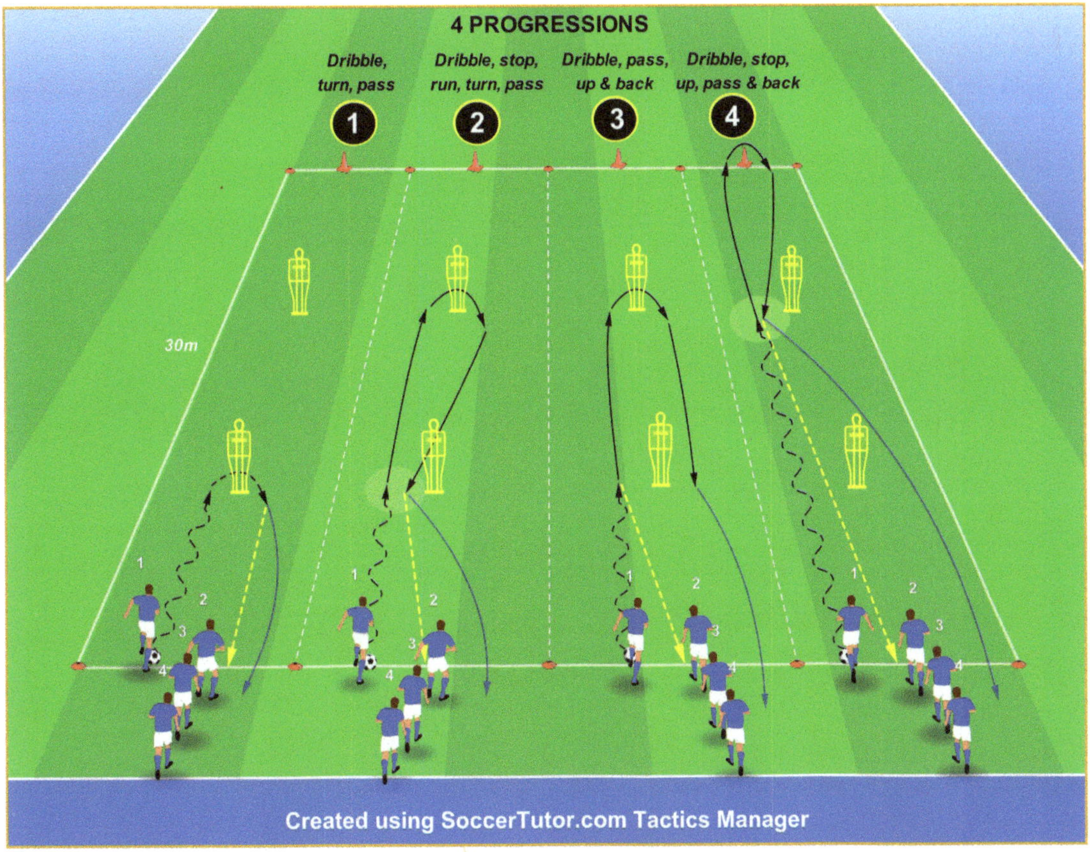

OBJECTIVE: Speed with accelerations and decelerations (with and without the ball).

Players perform 4 reps of each progression.

- **PROGRESSION 1:** Dribble ball around first mannequin, turn, and pass to next player waiting, jog back.

- **PROGRESSION 2:** Dribble to mannequin, stop, run around second mannequin, run back, pass back, then jog back to start.

- **PROGRESSION 3:** Dribble to first mannequin, turn, pass back, run around second mannequin, and jog back to start.

- **PROGRESSION 4:** Dribble to second mannequin, stop, run around end cone, run back, pass back, and then jog back to start.

Duration	Reps	Sets	Numbers	Size (m)	Work Duration
12 min	4	4	16-20	30 x 30	5-6 min

Speed Endurance Warm Ups

Speed Endurance 8. Progressive Overload Speed and Agility Exercises Circuit Training

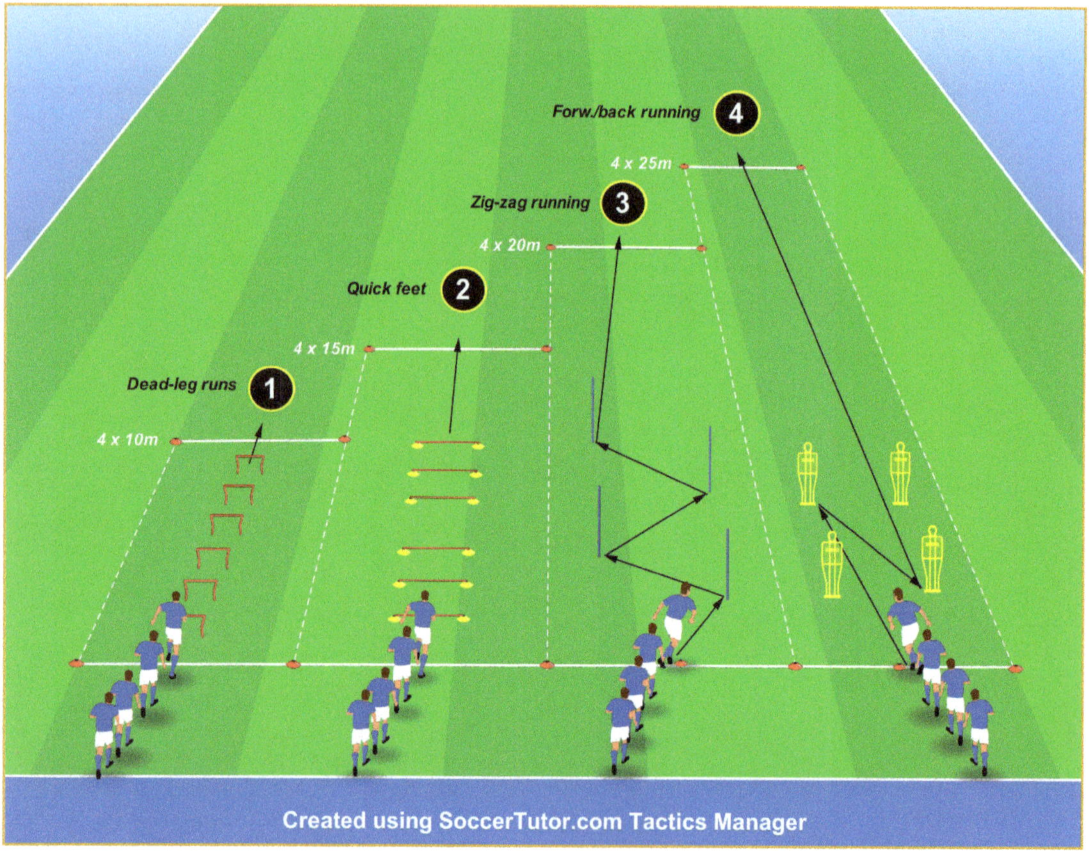

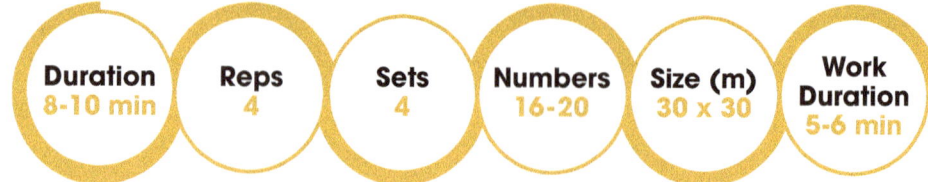

Duration	Reps	Sets	Numbers	Size (m)	Work Duration
8-10 min	4	4	16-20	30 x 30	5-6 min

OBJECTIVE: Coordination, agility, dynamic movement, and speed endurance training.

Players perform 4 reps of each progression.

PROGRESSION 1:
- "Dead-leg" running through 6 hurdles (4 reps x 10m).

PROGRESSION 2:
- Quick feet through 2 sets of 3 low ground hurdles (4 reps x 15m).

PROGRESSION 3:
- Zig-zag pattern running through 4 poles (4 reps x 20m).

PROGRESSION 4:
- Run forward to front left mannequin, diagonal back to back right mannequin, then sprint forward (4 reps x 25m).

Warm Ups to Maximise Performance

Speed Endurance Warm Ups

Speed Endurance 9. Agility, Coordination, and Speed 4-Station "Pyramid" Circuit Training

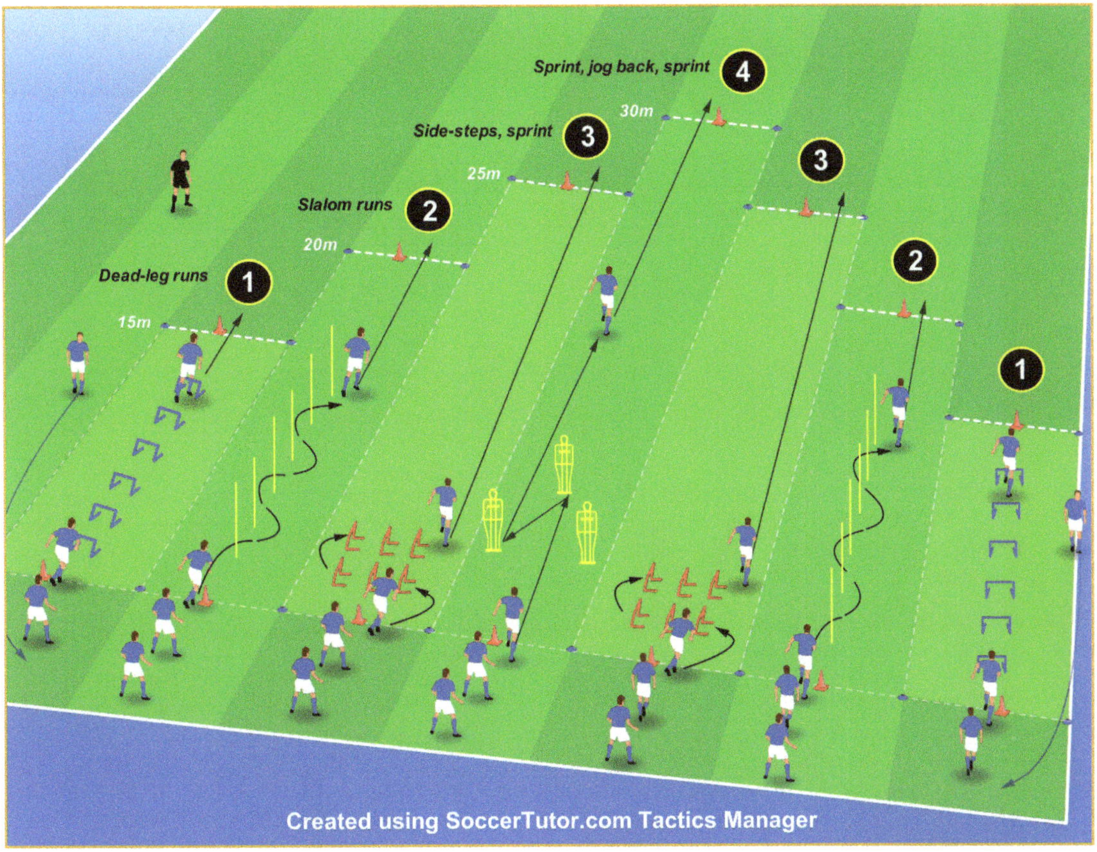

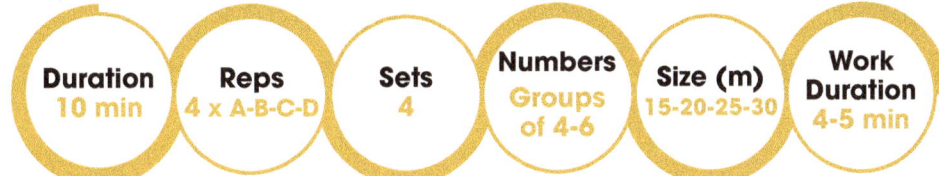

Duration	Reps	Sets	Numbers	Size (m)	Work Duration
10 min	4 x A-B-C-D	4	Groups of 4-6	15-20-25-30	4-5 min

OBJECTIVE: Agility, coordination, speed, mobility, strength, and flexibility.

The squad splits across the 7 stations but only perform reps of stations 1 → 2 → 3 → 4.

This warm up practice consists of 4 different exercise stations to work through:

1. Dead-leg runs through 6 hurdles (15m).
2. Slalom runs through 6 poles (20m).
3. Side-steps through 6 hurdles (25m).
4. Sprint, diagonal backward jog, and sprint to far cone (30m).

→ After each station, walk back to the start to recover. The players perform 4 reps at each station before moving to the next one.

REACTION SPEED WARM UPS

Reaction Speed Warm Ups

Reaction Speed Warm Up Practices

In this training methodology, the **Reaction Speed Warm Up Practices are strategically applied on days with reduced fatigue in training**. It is crucial when emphasising fast cognitive reactions and tactical scenarios, especially with increased recovery intervals.

The need arises on **smaller pitch days, prioritising quick decision making** over physical speed (Owen et al., 2016). **Coaches taper the load on these days**, prioritising freshness over fitness, as detailed in the *"Football Periodization" book (see pages 10-11 for details)*.

Strategic Implementation

Reduced Training Intensity and Fatigue on Cognitive-Intensive Days

Strategically using reaction-based warm ups is crucial on days with **reduced training intensity and fatigue-inducing elements**. Coaches may incorporate **more recovery bouts and coaching periods** to create a thought-provoking environment, emphasising **fast cognitive reactions and quick decision making**.

The smaller pitch or reduced training area heightens the need for quick cognitive processing in close encounters with opponents.

Decision Making Impact

These warm ups intentionally emphasise cognitive decision-making, preparing players for the training session by **reducing high speed running**.

Players must **think quickly and make accurate decisions**, engaging in scenarios that demand mental responsiveness.

Reduced Fatigue and Enhanced Cognitive Speed

In contrast to warm ups focusing on physical load, **reaction warm ups trigger specific movement patterns but minimise fatigue**. They strategically challenge players cognitively, promoting decision making and reactive elements, stimulating mental sharpness whilst minimising the physical load.

Optimising Cognitive Readiness

To conclude, the *Reaction Speed Warm Up* strategically aligns with the session focus in this methodology, optimising cognitive readiness without adding pre-training fatigue. **By minimising fatigue elements and prioritising fast cognitive reactions, coaches create an environment for quick decision-making**.

These warm ups acknowledge that **cognitive readiness is as vital as physical preparedness in football at all levels**.

Reaction Speed Warm Ups

Key Information

Warm ups can both reduce injury and improve performance. It is extremely important that exercise professionals use a well-designed warm up if they are to maximise the athletic potential of their athletes.

RAMP Protocol

 The RAMP framework allows activities to be easily classified and constructed in the following warm up sequence:

Raise
 Body temperature, heart rate, respiration rate, blood flow, and joint viscosity.

Activate & Mobilise
 Activate key muscles and mobilise key joints.

Potentiate
 Reach the same intensity of subsequent exercise and utilise post activation potentiation if applicable.

Time in Warm Up

 A 15 minute warm up 4 times per week over 12 weeks = 12 hours of training time.

Warm Up Effects

 Include but are not limited to:

- ↑ Strength and power
- ↑ Rate of force development
- ↑ Reaction time
- ↑ Muscle contraction and relaxation speed
- ↑ Blood to muscles
- ↑ Oxygen delivery

Our Summary

 Planning the warm up should be given as much attention as the main training content itself. Warm ups should not only be tailored to each training session or competition, but also to each athlete's highly-specific strengths and weaknesses.

Reaction Speed Warm Ups

2 DAYS UNTIL MATCH (MD +5/-2)
Unit Principle Training and Reaction Speed Development

Duration	45 min	70-75 min	85-95 min	60-70 min	45-60 min	90 min
Daily Theme	Recovery	Resistance	Speed Endurance	REACTION SPEED	Pre-Match Activation	Match
Preparation	Match Day (MD) +2/-5	Match Day (MD) +3/-4	Match Day (MD) +4/-3	Match Day (MD) +5/-2	Match Day (MD) +6/-1	Match Day
		Positional Principles	Collective Principles	Unit Principles		
Game Type Focus	-	SSGs 1v1-4v4 (+GKs) Small Area	LSGs 8v8-10v10 (+GKs) Large Area	MSGs 5v5-7v7 (+GKs) Medium Area	LSGs 8v8-10v10 (+GKs) Small/Med Area	Match Day 11v11
Bout Durations	-	1-3 min	5-10 min	3-5 min	4 min	2 x 45 min
	Mon: Recovery	Tue-Wed: Conditioning		Thu-Fri: Preparation		Perform

* **Training Week based on Professional Microcycle Example** - see pages 20-21.

Key Focus on:
- **Unit Based Principles**
- **Near Maximum Acceleration Efforts**
- **Agility Based Content**

Reaction Speed Warm Ups

REACTION SPEED TRAINING SESSION
2 Days Until Match (MD +5/-2)

Unit Principle Training and Reaction Speed (60-70 min):

1. Reaction Speed Warm Up (5-7 min)
2. Intensive Technical Practice (10-15 min)
3. Reaction Speed Conditioning Practice (5-15 min)
4. Medium Sided Possession (6-15 min)
5. Medium Sided Game in Large Area (10-25 min)

Reaction Speed Warm Ups

2 DAYS UNTIL MATCH (MD +5/-2)
Reaction Speed Warm Up Practices

INTENSITY: All practices are performed at full intensity

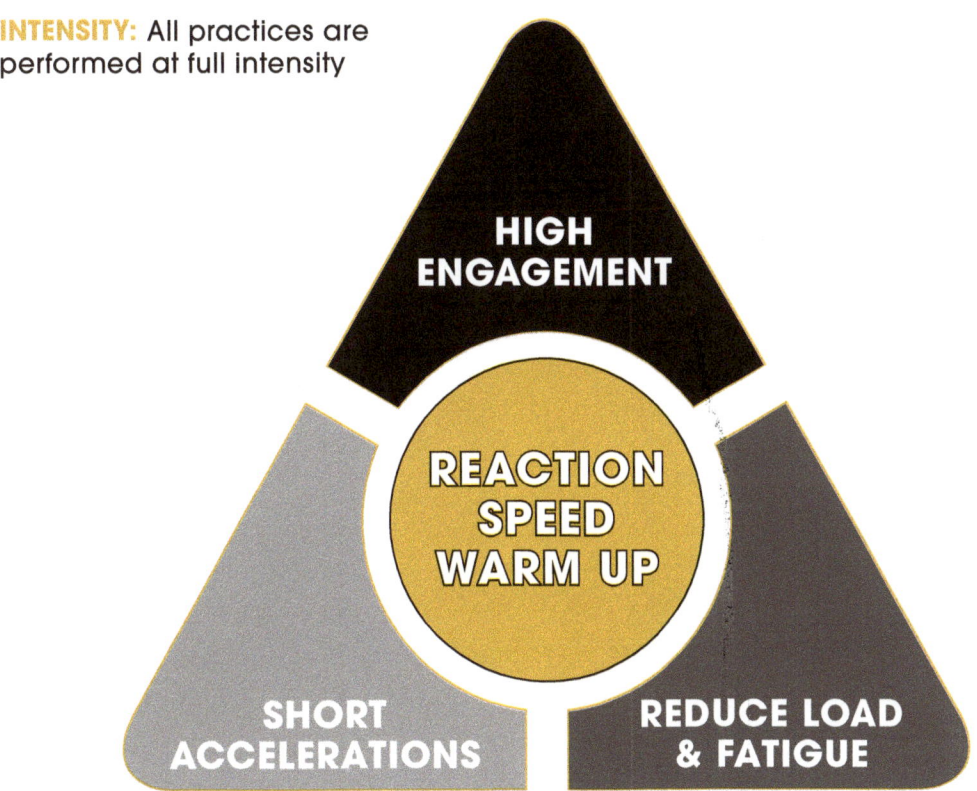

What are Reaction Speed Warm Ups?
- Inclusive of lots of reaction based work.
- The focus is to move quickly from a physical perspective but also react fast.
- Includes lots of shorter acceleration based work but reduced aggressive decelerations.

Why are they used on this day of the training week (MD +5/-2)?
- Reaction speed warm ups are used on this training day as the key is to try and reduce fatigue in the players' legs whilst remaining engaged to react quickly from a psychological perspective.

How does this help to maximise performance?
- Reaction speed warm ups are used on this day as a way of reducing the load based on the previous two training days being of a higher training load volume.

Reaction Speed Warm Ups

Reaction Speed 1. Quick Footwork and Coordination Warm Up Exercises

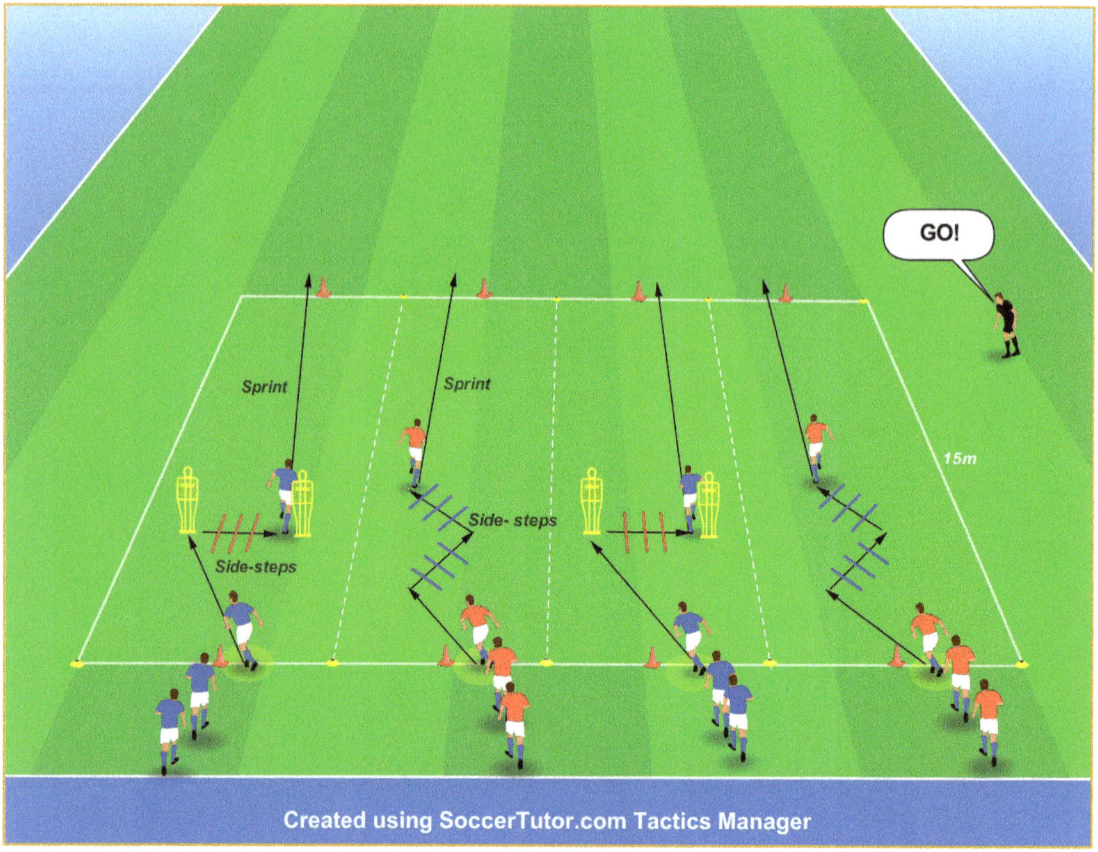

Duration	Reps	Sets	Numbers	Size (m)	Work Duration
5-10 min	4 x 15 m	4	Groups of 4-6	15 x 30	4-5 min

OBJECTIVE: Speed, balance, agility, quick footwork, and coordination.

This is a warm up practice that focuses on quickness of movement with 2 continuous stations to work through:

1. Run to mannequin → Side-steps through ground poles → Sprint to cone → Walk back.

2. Side-steps through ground poles (zig-zag) → Sprint to cone → Walk back.

Reaction Speed Warm Ups

Reaction Speed 2. "Rebounding" Changes of Direction and Agility Warm Up Circuit

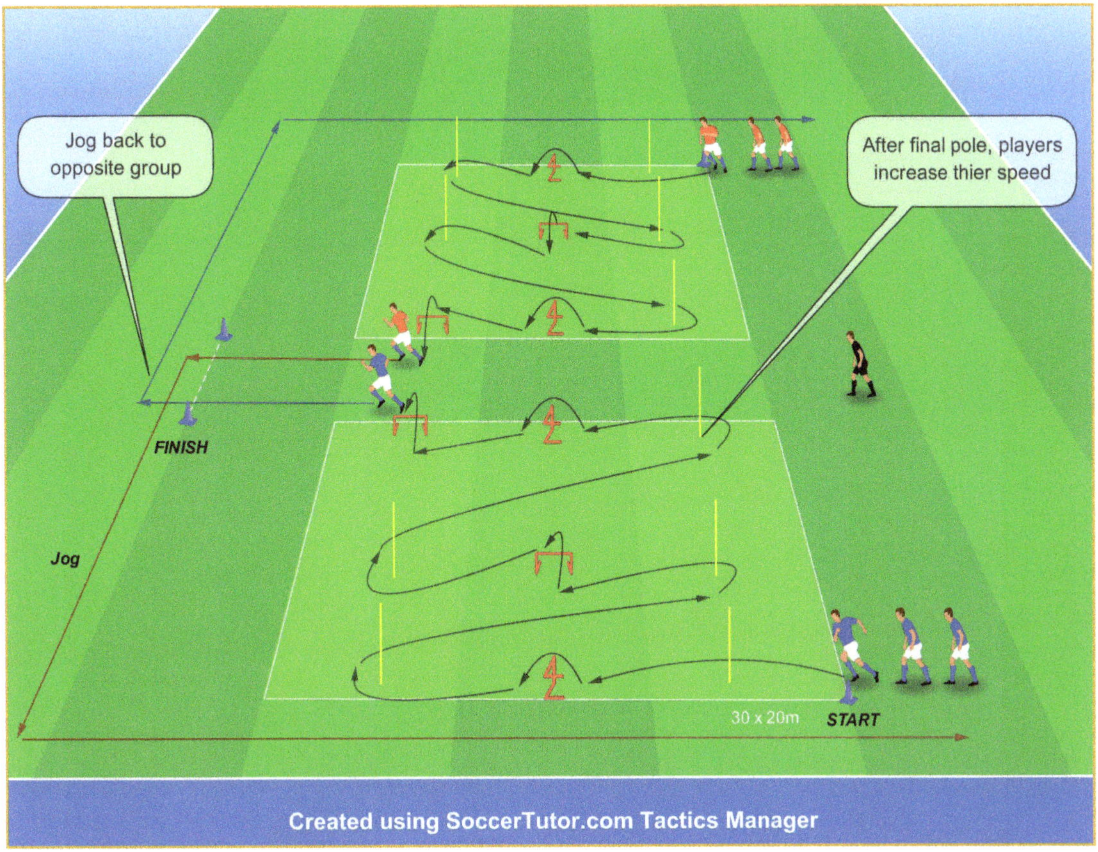

Duration	Reps	Sets	Numbers	Size (m)	Work Duration
8-10 min	4	4	Groups of 4-10	30 x 20	4-6 min

OBJECTIVE: Dynamic flexibility, agility, movement, and changes of direction at speed.

Each rep (start to finish) is approximately 15 seconds.

- The players move around the poles in the circuit, jumping over the hurdles.
- They move in various directions (forward, backward, sideways) from pole to pole.
- After moving around the final pole, the players increase their speed slightly over the last 2 hurdles.
- They finish by sprinting in between the 2 blue cones and jogging to the back of the other group.

Reaction Speed Warm Ups

Reaction Speed 3. Agility Exercises with Fast Feet and Changes of Direction Warm Up

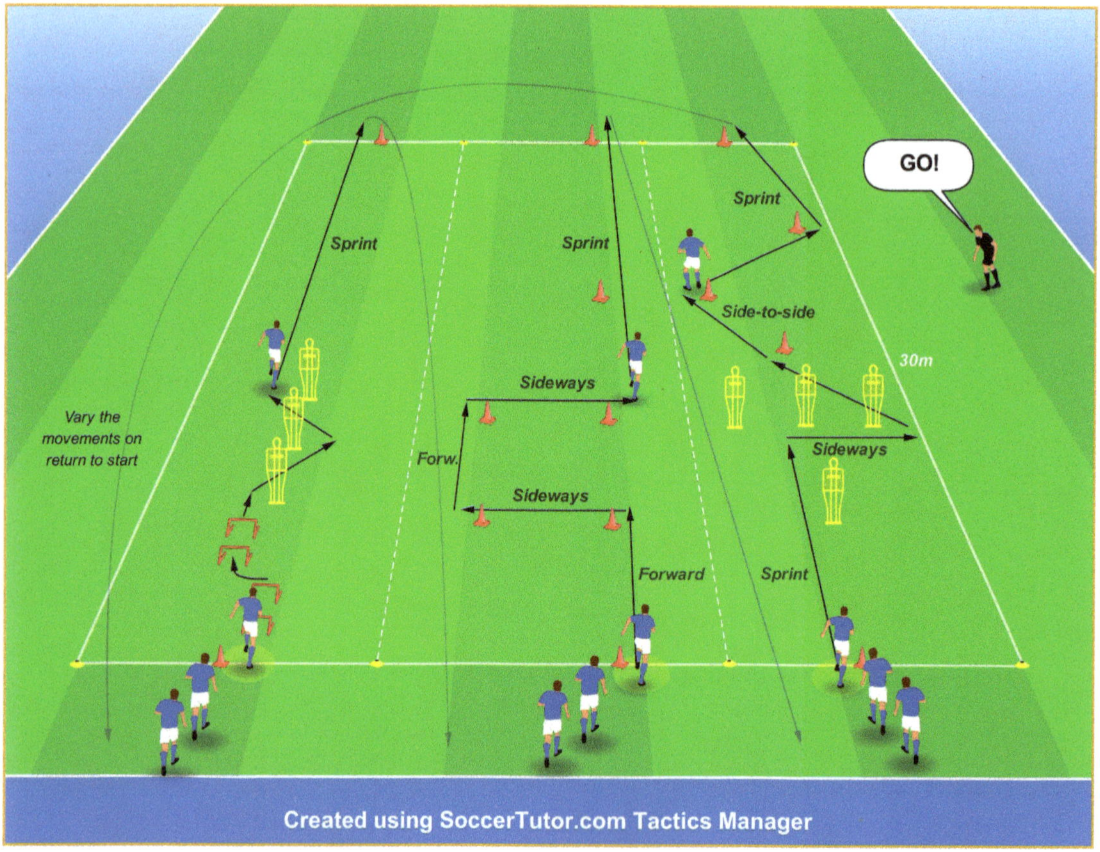

Duration	Reps	Sets	Numbers	Size (m)	Work Duration
10-12 min	30 m	8-10	Groups of 4-5	30 x 25	5-6 min

OBJECTIVE: Coordination, agility, and speed with changes of direction.

Split into 3 stations, the players perform various agility and speed exercises through the equipment which is set out.

Once they have completed the agility work, they walk to join the next station.

1. Low hurdles → Zig-Zag through mannequins → Sprint to cone.

2. Forward → Sideways → Forward → Sideways → Sprint to end cone.

3. Sprint → Sideways → Diagonal → Side-to-side through cones → Sprint to end cone.

COACHING POINTS: High intensity throughout, quick feet, good balance.

Reaction Speed Warm Ups

Reaction Speed 4. Quick Footwork and Coordination Diamond Warm Up Circuit

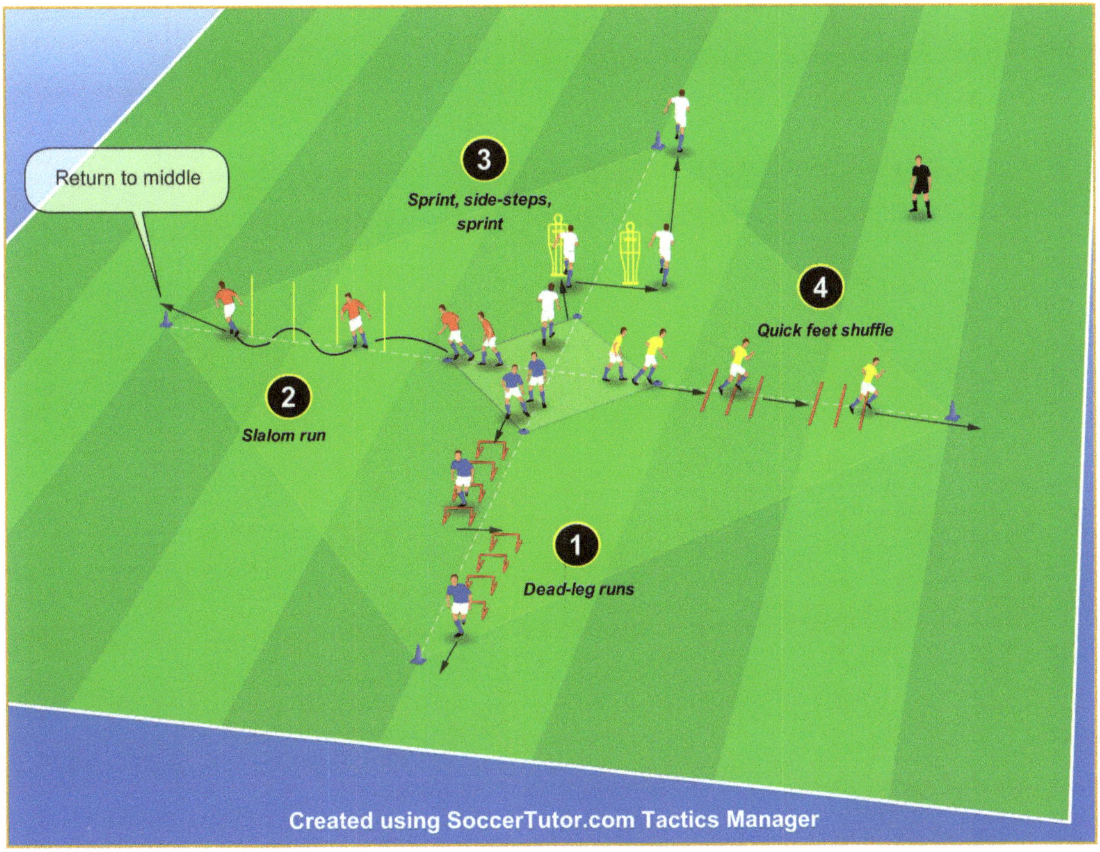

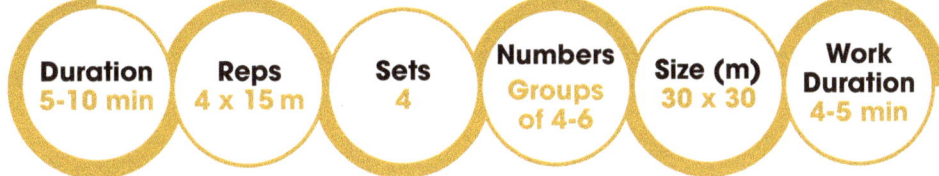

Duration	Reps	Sets	Numbers	Size (m)	Work Duration
5-10 min	4 x 15 m	4	Groups of 4-6	30 x 30	4-5 min

OBJECTIVE: Speed, balance, agility, quick footwork, and coordination.

This is a warm up practice that focuses on quickness of movement with 4 continuous 12 metre exercise stations to work through:

1. Dead-leg runs through 2 sets of 4 hurdles → Back to middle.
2. Slalom run through poles → Back to middle.
3. Sprint to 1st mannequin → Side-steps to 2nd mannequin → Sprint to cone → Back to middle.
4. Quick feet shuffle through 2 sets of 3 ground poles → Sprint to cone → Back to middle.

©SOCCERTUTOR.COM

Warm Ups to Maximise Performance

Reaction Speed Warm Ups

Reaction Speed 5. Various 2-Footed Juggling Techniques Circle Warm Up

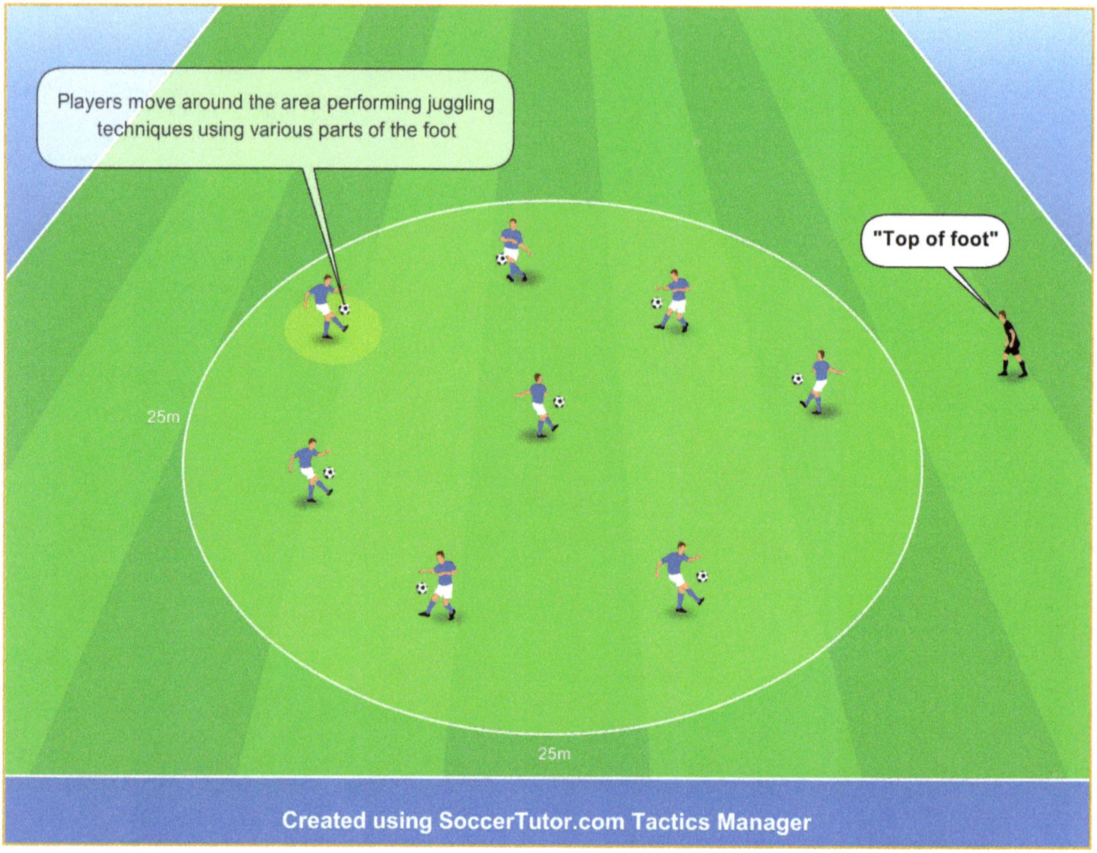

Duration	Reps	Sets	Numbers	Size (m)	Work Duration
10-12 min	30 sec	8	1-20	25	5-6 min

OBJECTIVE: Warm up with skills to develop aerial ball control (juggling).

Players move around the area performing various juggling techniques using various parts of the foot:

1. Top left foot / right foot.
2. Inside left foot / right foot.
3. Outside left foot / right foot.
4. Left foot + thigh.
5. Right foot + thigh.
6. Left foot + chest.
7. Right foot + chest.
8. High volleys (right and left foot).

Reaction Speed Warm Ups

Reaction Speed 6. Technical Running With the Ball Quick Footwork at Speed Warm Up

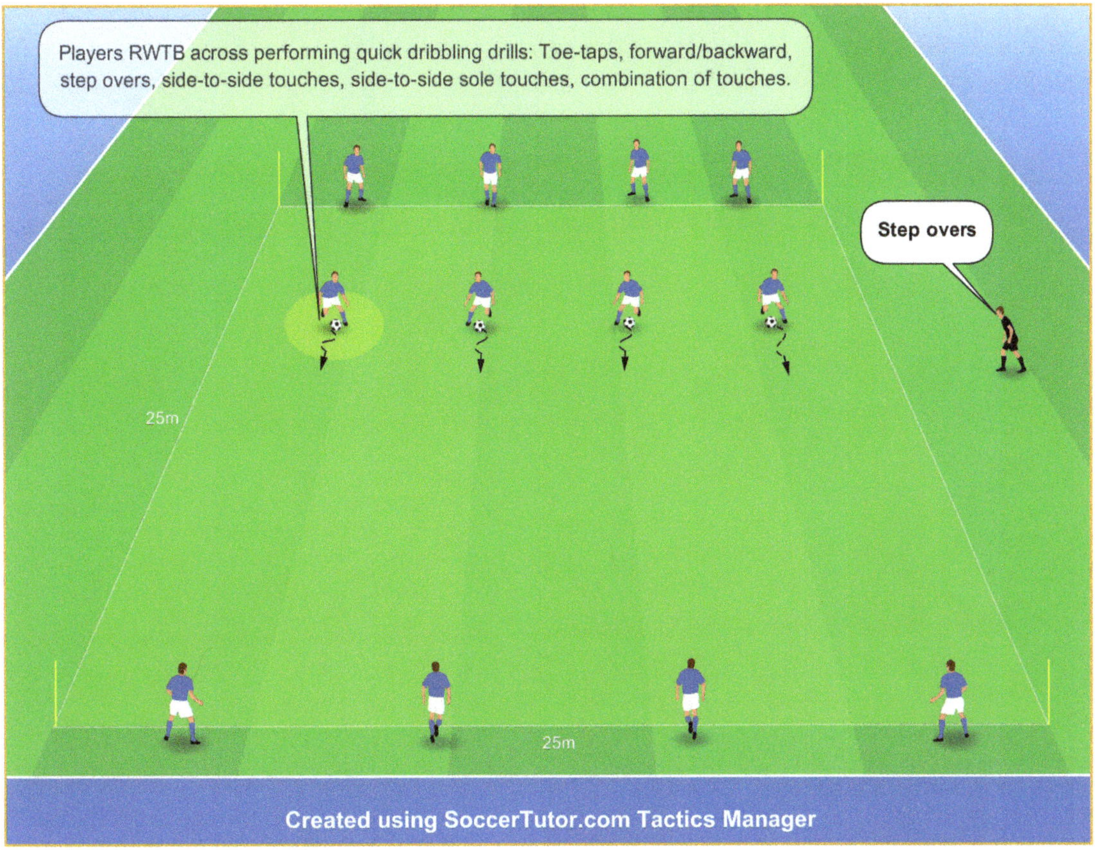

Players RWTB across performing quick dribbling drills: Toe-taps, forward/backward, step overs, side-to-side touches, side-to-side sole touches, combination of touches.

Step overs

25m

25m

Duration	Reps	Sets	Numbers	Size (m)	Work Duration
10 min	25 m	8-12	Groups of 3-4	25 x 25	3-4 min

OBJECTIVE: Warm up with skills to develop ball control and dribbling (at speed).

- All players have a ball each. They **run with the ball (RWTB)** across the area performing various quick dribbling drills.
- The skills included are toe-taps, forward/backward, step overs, side-to-side touches, side-to-side sole touches, combination of touches, etc.
- As soon as the first player reaches the end, the next player waiting on the other side goes with the same ball.
- The emphasis is placed on quick footwork with many touches and speed across the area.

Reaction Speed Warm Ups

Reaction Speed 7. Ball Control, Skills, and Quick Reactions to Commands Warm Up

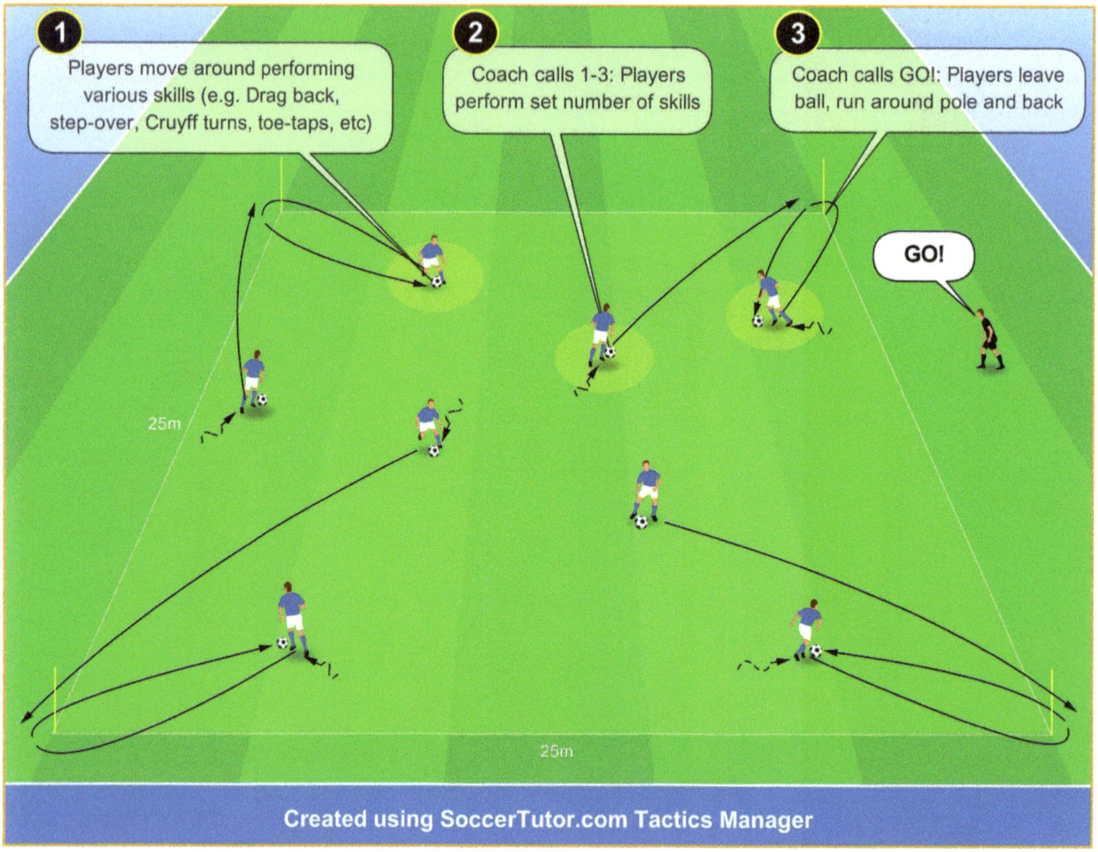

1. Players move around performing various skills (e.g. Drag back, step-over, Cruyff turns, toe-taps, etc)

2. Coach calls 1-3: Players perform set number of skills

3. Coach calls GO!: Players leave ball, run around pole and back

Duration	Reps	Sets	Numbers	Size (m)	Work Duration
5-10 min	30 sec - 1 min	7-8	Groups of 8-12	25 x 25	5-6 min

OBJECTIVE: Technical ball control, turns, quick reactions, and speed.

- The players move around the area with the ball performing various skills (e.g. drag back, step-over, Cruyff turns, toe-taps, etc).
- On the coach's call (1-3), they perform a set number of skills (e.g. **1** = 5 step overs, **2** = 10 toes-taps, **3** = 3 drag backs).
- When the coach calls "**Go!**", the players leave their balls inside the area and run around a corner pole, then back to their ball.
- The practice should also involve a series of dynamic flexibility and static stretches.

Reaction Speed Warm Ups

Reaction Speed 8. "The Clock" Running Inside and Out Dynamic Warm Up

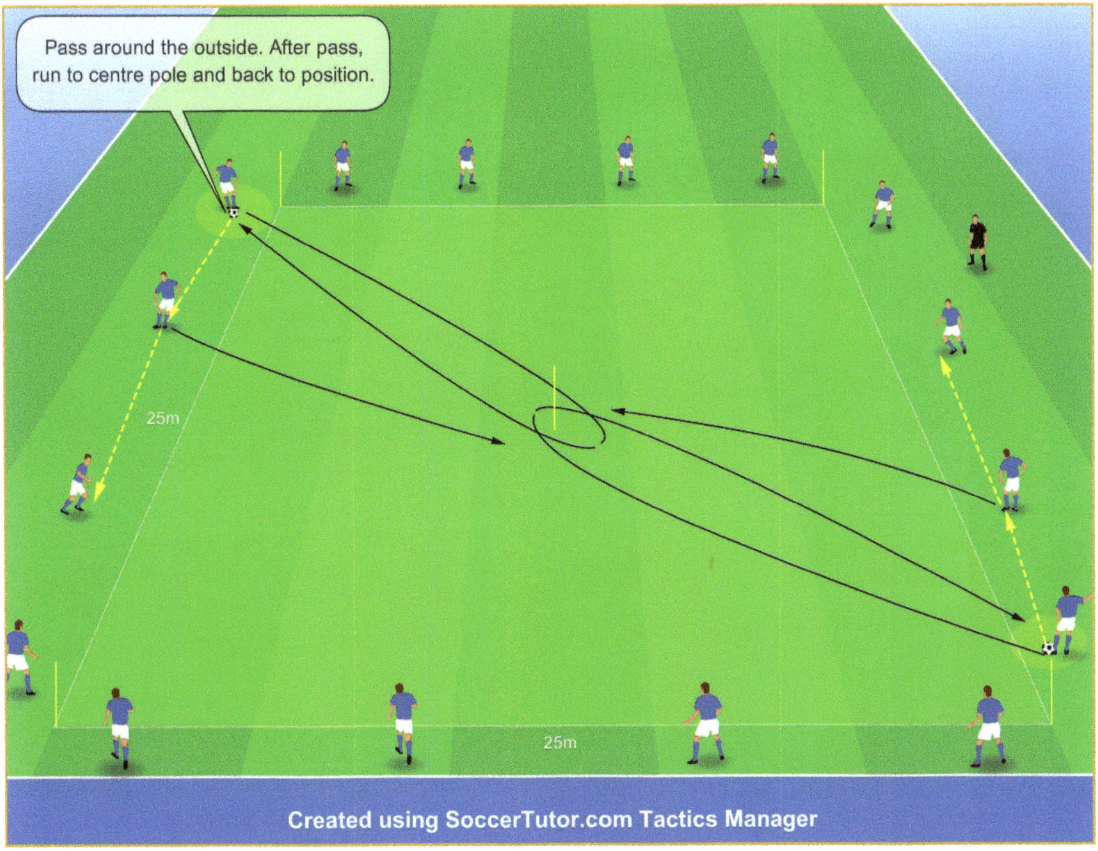

Pass around the outside. After pass, run to centre pole and back to position.

Duration	Reps	Sets	Numbers	Size (m)	Work Duration
8-10 min	2 min	4-6	Groups of 16-20	25 x 25	5-6 min

OBJECTIVE: Acceleration, deceleration, changes of direction, and agility.

- The players pass around the outside. After a pass, they run to the centre pole and back to their position. The coach can involve different types of movement (backward, sideways, jockeying etc). Also, vary the types of passes by missing players out, introduce skills (turns), or players perform a roll in the centre.

- **PROGRESSION:** Add more balls to raise the tempo of the session.
- **NOTE:** Throughout the warm up, the players also perform various dynamic flexibility movements into the centre pole and back out when the coach instructs them to do so.

Reaction Speed Warm Ups

Reaction Speed 9. Zig-Zag Dribbling and Finishing at Speed Technical Warm Up

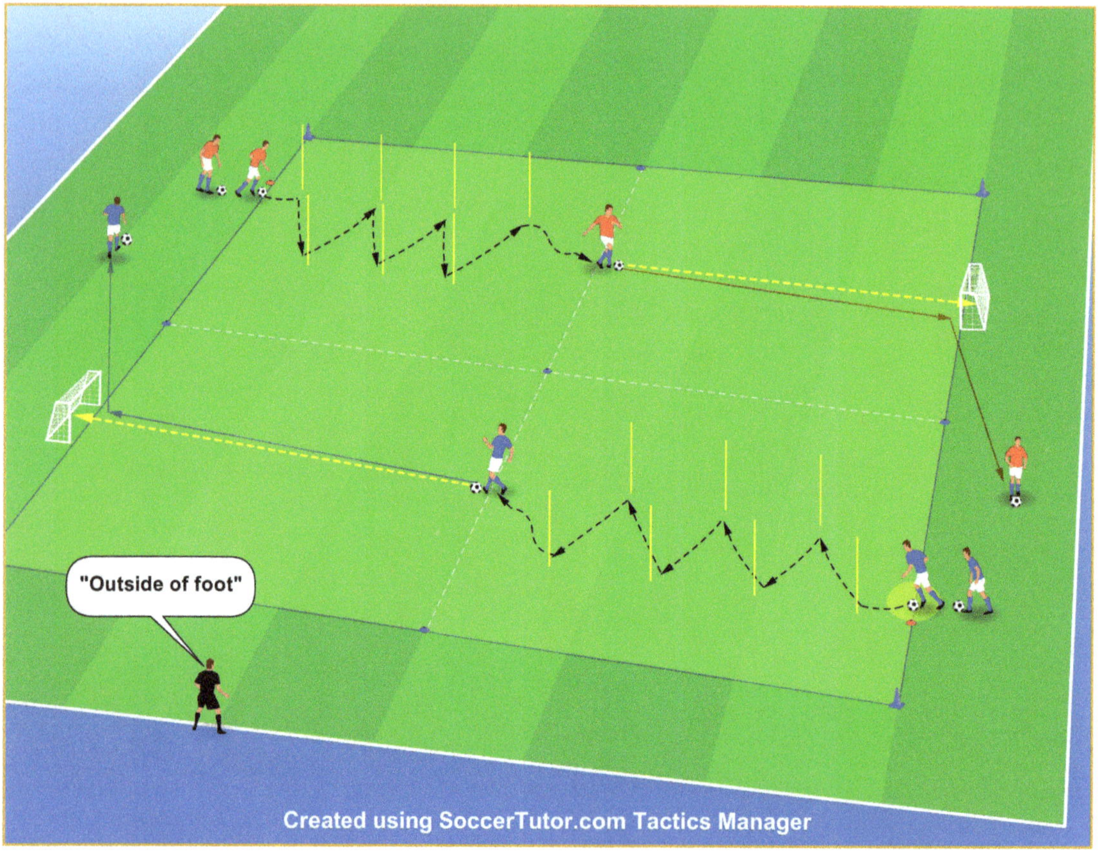

[Diagram showing a 25x25 training area with zig-zag pole setup, two small goals, and players dribbling through poles. Label: "Outside of foot". Created using SoccerTutor.com Tactics Manager]

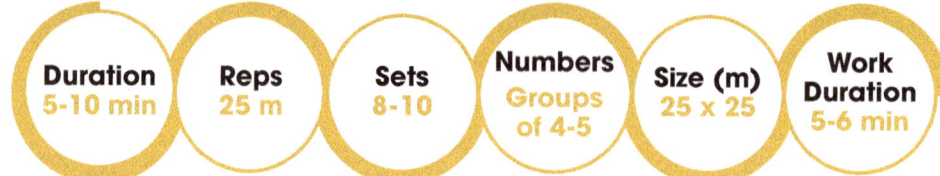

Duration	Reps	Sets	Numbers	Size (m)	Work Duration
5-10 min	25 m	8-10	Groups of 4-5	25 x 25	5-6 min

OBJECTIVE: Warm up with skills to develop close ball control and ball striking.

Players move with the ball from pole to pole in a zig-zag pattern performing various skills:

1. Cutting inside (both feet).
2. Outside of foot (both feet).
3. Inside/outside (both feet).
4. Cutting away (both feet).
5. Drag + change direction.
6. Drag + through (Cruyff turn).

→ When players come off the last pole, they pass into the small goal and join the other group.

→ Build the intensity across the reps.

Warm Ups to Maximise Performance

Reaction Speed Warm Ups

Reaction Speed 10. Coordination and Agility with One-Two Combination Warm Up

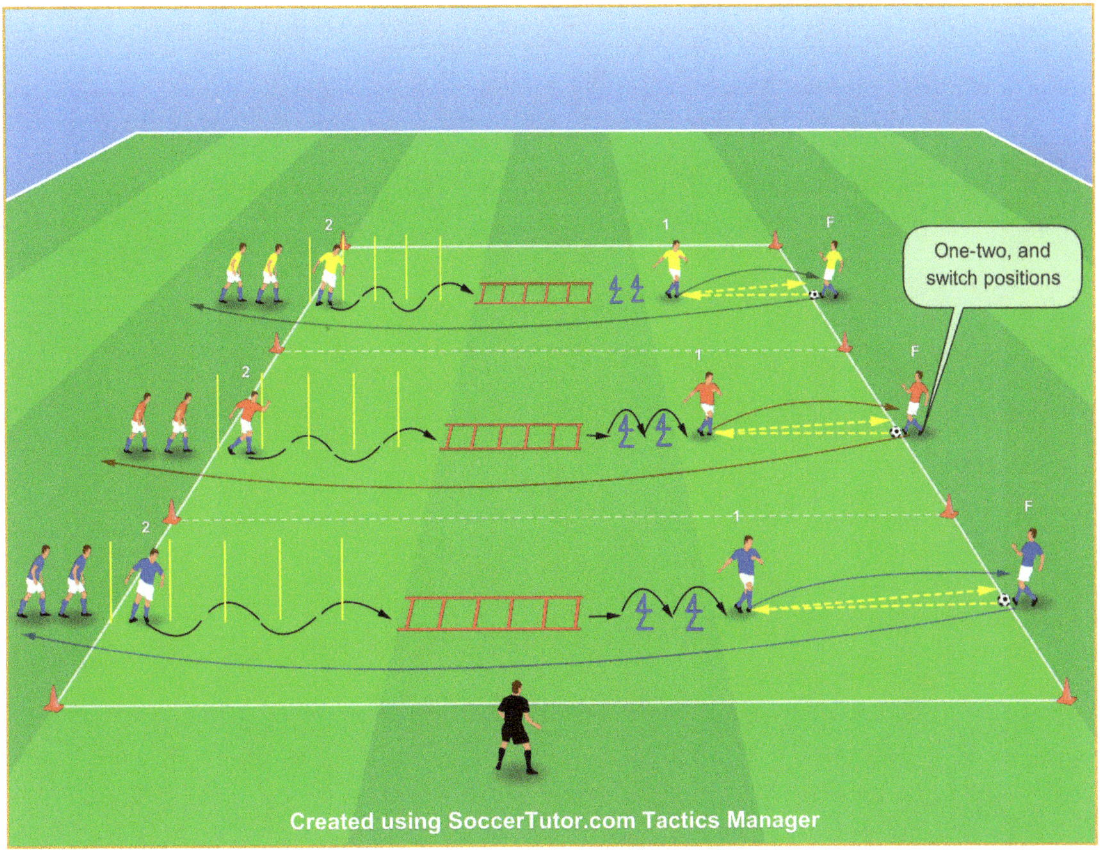

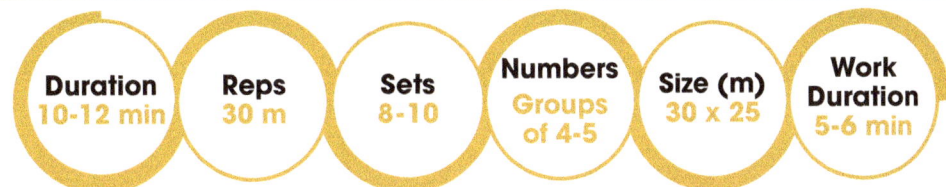

Duration	Reps	Sets	Numbers	Size (m)	Work Duration
10-12 min	30 m	8-10	Groups of 4-5	30 x 25	5-6 min

OBJECTIVE: Speed, coordination, balance, agility, passing, and receiving.

1. **Player 1** runs through the poles (zig-zag).
2. Step through the ladder performing movements determined by the coach.
3. Jump over the 2 hurdles.
4. Play a one-two combination with the feeder player.
5. **Player 1** moves to **Player 2's** position. **Player 2** jogs to the back of the group.

→ Include continuous exercise with static and dynamic stretches in between repetitions. Slowly increase the intensity. The players perform at 85-95% of maximum heart rate (HRM).

Reaction Speed Warm Ups

Reaction Speed 11. Agility Exercises + One-Two in Multi-Station Warm Up (1)

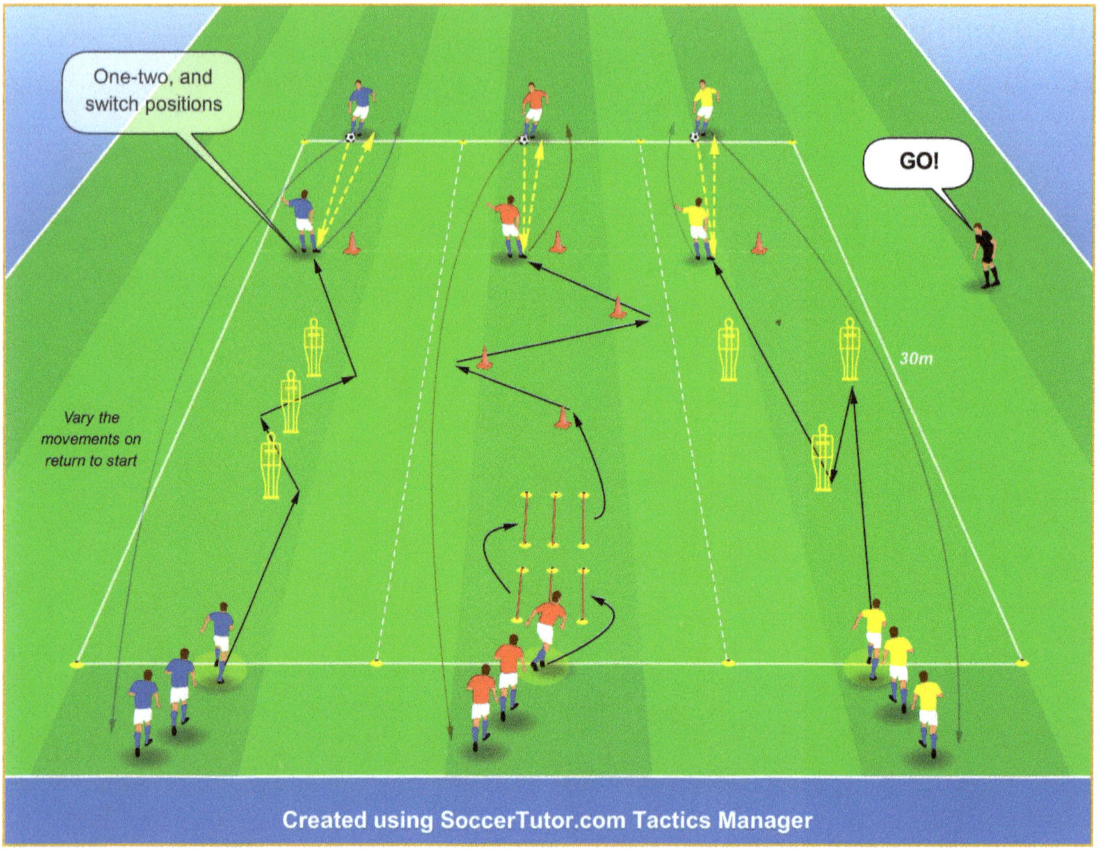

One-two, and switch positions

GO!

Vary the movements on return to start

30m

Duration	Reps	Sets	Numbers	Size (m)	Work Duration
10-12 min	30 m	8-10	Groups of 4-5	30 x 25	5-6 min

OBJECTIVE: Speed, coordination, agility, passing, and receiving.

- Within each station, we start with 4 players at the bottom without a ball and a 5th player at the top with a ball.

- On the coach's instruction, the players without balls in all 3 groups perform various agility and speed exercises through the equipment which is set out.

- Once they have completed the agility work, they play a one-two at the top, and switch positions with the server. The next player then goes.

- Assign an amount of reps before the groups rotate to the next station and change the servers often.

Reaction Speed Warm Ups

Reaction Speed 12. Agility Exercises + One-Two in Multi-Station Warm Up (2)

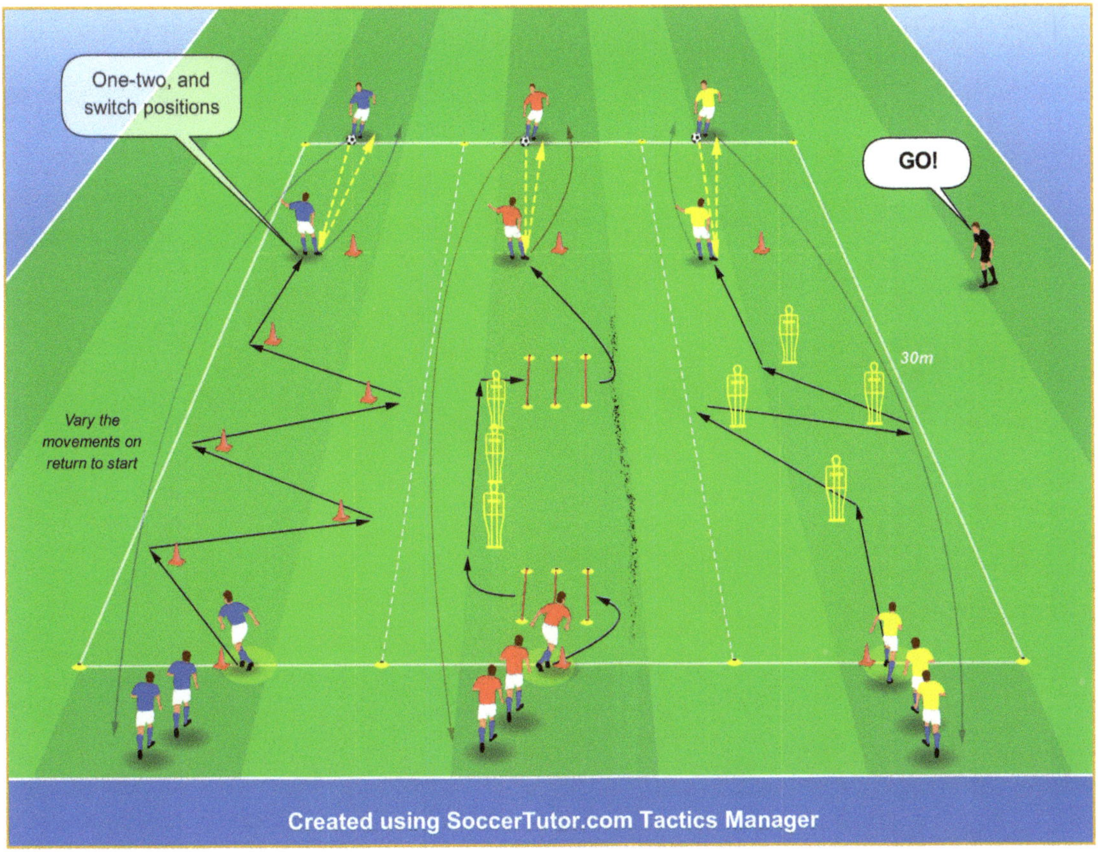

One-two, and switch positions

Vary the movements on return to start

GO!

30m

Created using SoccerTutor.com Tactics Manager

Duration	Reps	Sets	Numbers	Size (m)	Work Duration
10-12 min	30 m	8-10	Groups of 4-5	30 x 25	5-6 min

OBJECTIVE: Speed, coordination, agility, passing, and receiving.

- Within each station, we start with 4 players at the bottom without a ball and a 5th player at the top with a ball.
- On the coach's instruction, the players without balls in all 3 groups perform various agility and speed exercises through the equipment which is set out.
- Once they have completed the agility work, they play a one-two at the top, and switch positions with the server. The next player then goes.
- Assign an amount of reps before the groups rotate to the next station and change the servers often.

Reaction Speed Warm Ups

Reaction Speed 13. Lateral Coordination and Acceleration "Spin & Go" Warm Up

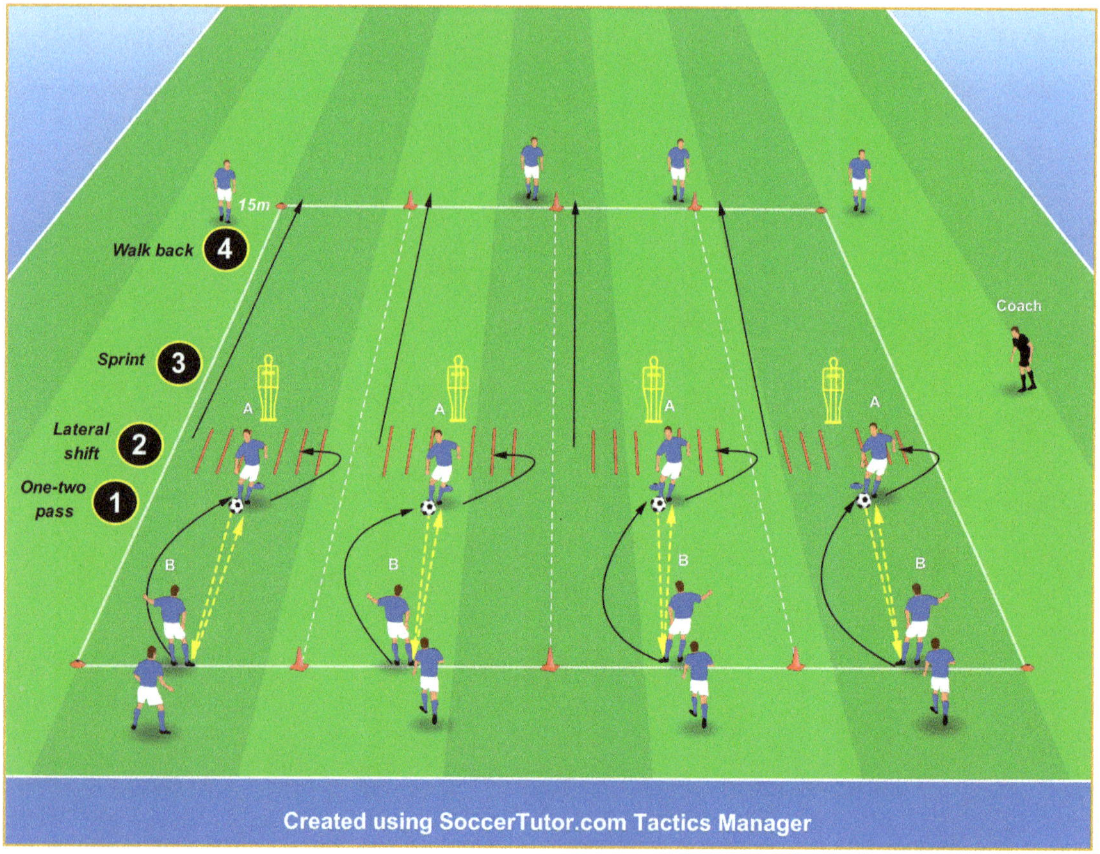

Duration	Reps	Sets	Numbers	Size (m)	Work Duration
5-10 min	4 x 15 m	4	Groups of 4-6	15 x 30	4-5 min

OBJECTIVE: Agility, coordination, passing, receiving, and acceleration speed.

The players are in groups as they perform the same reaction speed exercises and then walk back to the start (recover):

1. **Player A** starts with a ball on the cone and plays a one-two with **Player B**.
2. **Player A** spins around and uses side-steps through the ground poles.
3. Sprint to the far cone.
4. Walk back to the start.

→ The players rotate positions with **Player B** becoming the new **Player A**, and the next player waiting becoming the new **Player B**.

Reaction Speed Warm Ups

Reaction Speed 14. Speed, Coordination, and Awareness "Windows" Warm Up with One-Twos

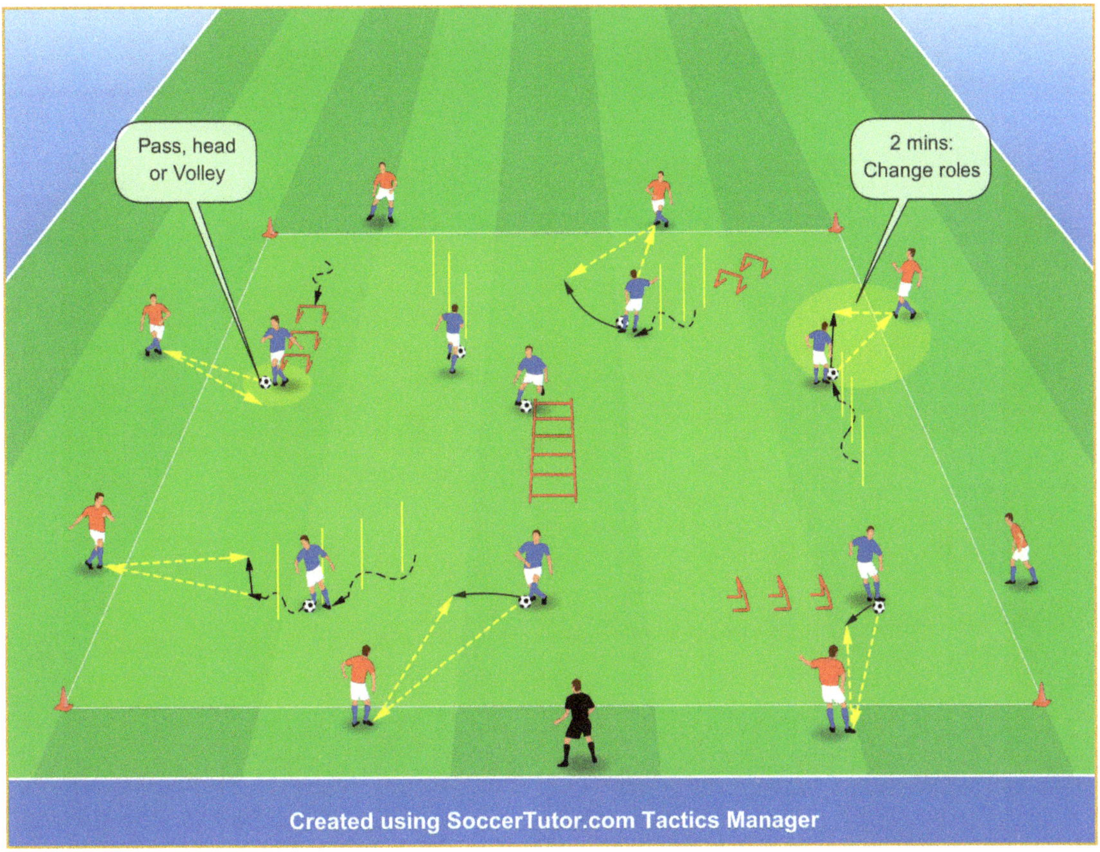

Duration	Reps	Sets	Numbers	Size (m)	Work Duration
12-15 min	30 sec	10	8-16	25 x 25	5 min

OBJECTIVE: Dynamic flexibility, agility, movement, passing, and receiving.

- Players perform various movements through the equipment laid out (backward, sideways, forward) and then move to a player on the outside of the square and play a one-two (volley, head, or pass), before moving through another piece of equipment.

- Ensure the players change roles with their partners after e.g. 2 minutes.
- **PROGRESSION:** The players move towards their partner on the outside and exchange 3 passes before changing roles (continually changing from inside to outside, and vice versa).

Reaction Speed Warm Ups

Reaction Speed 15. Passing and Reactions for Speed Work in a 4-Grid Warm Up

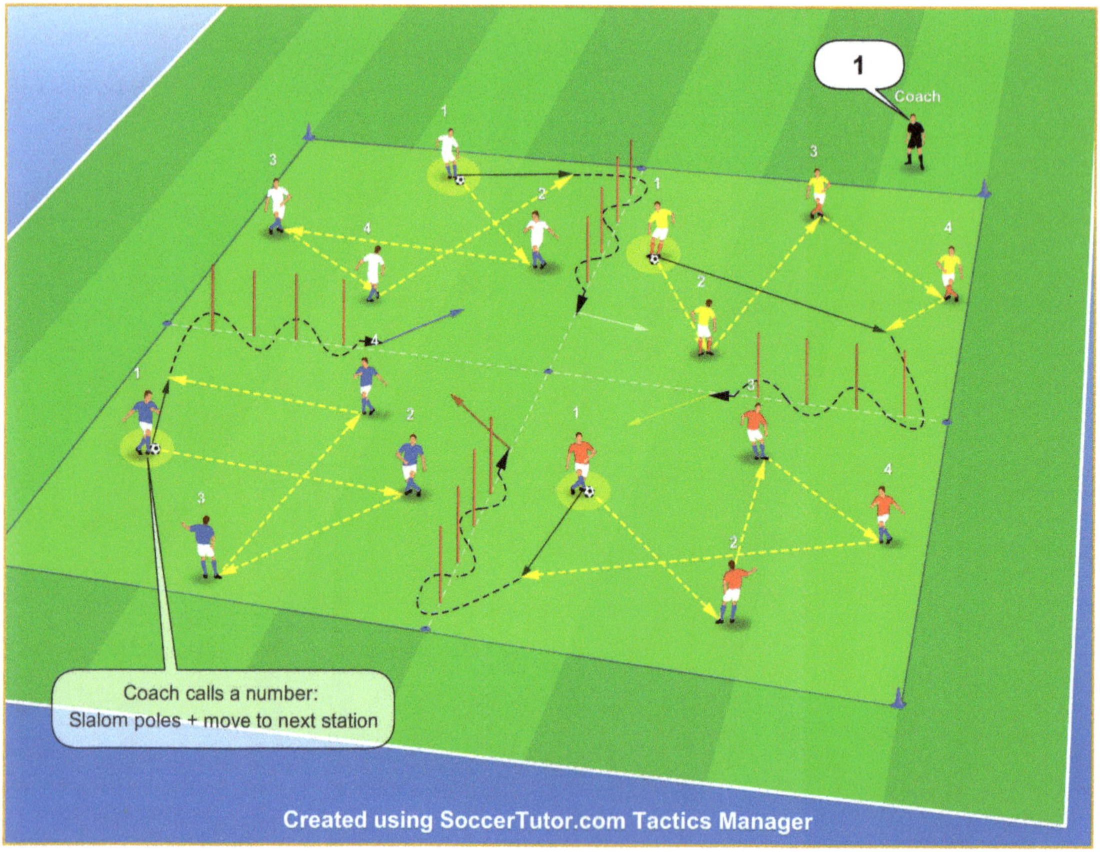

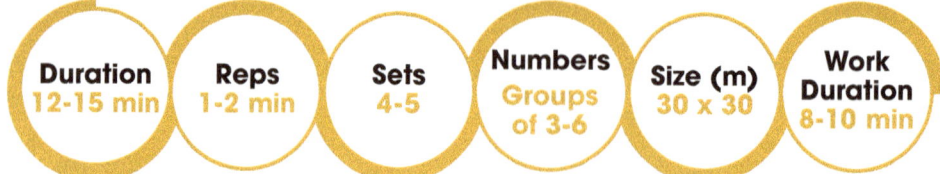

Coach calls a number:
Slalom poles + move to next station

Created using SoccerTutor.com Tactics Manager

Duration	Reps	Sets	Numbers	Size (m)	Work Duration
12-15 min	1-2 min	4-5	Groups of 3-6	30 x 30	8-10 min

OBJECTIVE: Passing, awareness, quick reactions, and speed work.

- The players are in groups and are all numbered 1-4. They start by passing to each other in that order 1 → 2 → 3 → 4.

- On the coach's call (**Nº 1 in diagram**), **Player 1** from each of the 4 groups leaves the area, slalom runs through the poles and joins the adjacent group (clockwise).

- The coach can call out any number at any time and can call more than one number.

- Work for the set duration and then do dynamic and static stretching.

- **PROGRESSION:** To raise the level of intensity, the players must run around a pole after every pass.

PRE-MATCH ACTIVATION WARM UPS

Pre-Match Activation Warm Ups

Pre-Match Activation Warm Ups (Training the Day Before Match)

In football preparation, the *Activation Warm Up* is vital, specifically reserved for match day minus one (MD-1) - the day before the match. The aim is similar to the previous section, with a **focus on minimising fatigue elements with a balanced warm up**.

Tailored for neural stimulation with **short, sharp movements and high-reactive elements, it avoids cognitive fatigue**.

This approach aims to create a positive mindset, ensuring a **relaxed and enjoyable atmosphere** as players prepare for the upcoming match day.

Short, Sharp Movements, and High Reactivity

- The activation warm up centres on short, sharp movements that stimulate neural pathways for rapid muscle activation.
- Designed to be highly reactive, it encourages **quick and efficient muscle engagement**.
- The **short duration ensures impact without causing undue fatigue**, striking a **balance between activation and energy preservation** for the match.

Balancing Fun and Relaxation

- Creating a fun, relaxed environment tailored to match day minus one (MD-1), the warm up incorporates elements of enjoyment.
- Encouraging players to relish the process should generate a positive mindset, team cohesion, and group spirit.
- This balance is crucial, setting the tone for the entire build-up to match day.

Preparing the Mind and Body for Performance

- Essentially, the *Activation Warm Up* is a strategic approach to prepare football players for match day.
- Strategically managing fatigue, emphasising short and sharp movements, and including **high-reactive elements** optimise players' physical and mental states.
- Incorporating fun and relaxation adds to a positive pre-match atmosphere, fostering **ideal conditions for peak performance**.

Pre-Match Activation Warm Ups

Effects of Warm Up, Post-Warm Up, and Re-Warm Up Strategies on Explosive Efforts in Team Sports

WARM UP & POST-WARM UP

Properly structured strategies in the warm up

Avoiding a long rest in the post-warm up

10-15 min
50-90% HRmax

Improved Explosive Performance

Studies tend to recommend a short active warm up strategy, gradually increasing intensity, and the use of heated garments soon after the warm up to maintain muscle temperature.

RE-WARM UP

2 minutes of active re-warm up with short-term sprints and jumps should be needed for transitions longer than 15 minutes (~90% of maximum heart rate).

HALF TIME RE-WARM UP

Combining heated garments to maintain muscle temperature.

Performing an active strategy, with explosive tasks or small sided games for 5 min before re-entering the game.

Results in better explosive performance than 15 min of resting.

Reference: Silva et al. Sports Med 2018

Pre-Match Activation Warm Ups

1 DAY UNTIL MATCH (MD +6/-1)
Pre-Match Activation Training Day

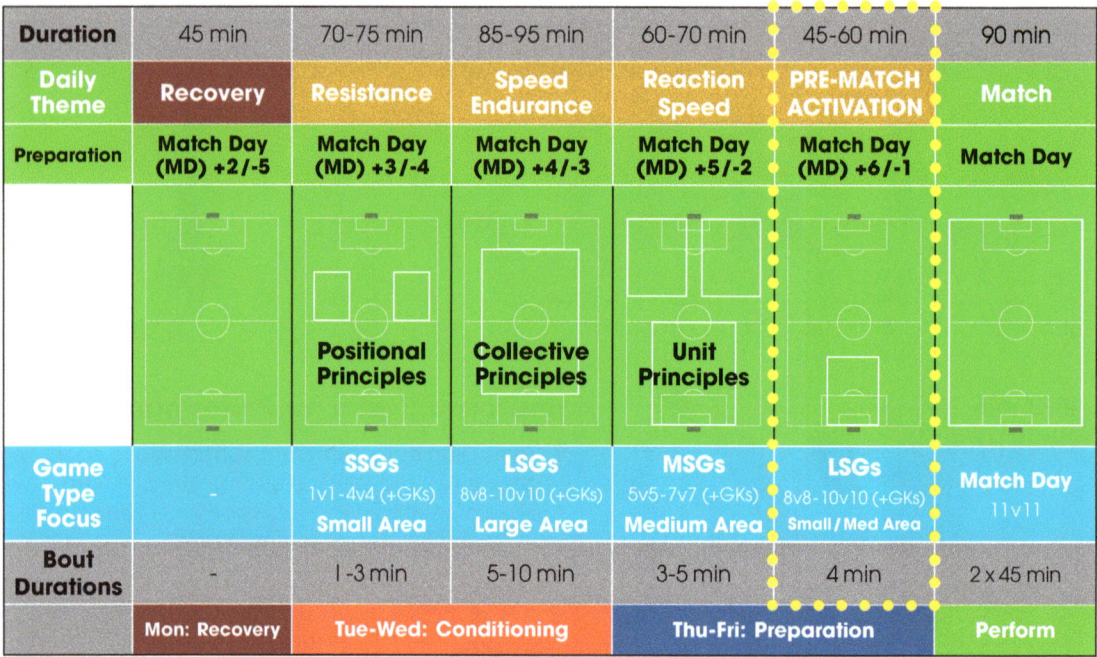

Duration	45 min	70-75 min	85-95 min	60-70 min	45-60 min	90 min
Daily Theme	Recovery	Resistance	Speed Endurance	Reaction Speed	PRE-MATCH ACTIVATION	Match
Preparation	Match Day (MD) +2/-5	Match Day (MD) +3/-4	Match Day (MD) +4/-3	Match Day (MD) +5/-2	Match Day (MD) +6/-1	Match Day
		Positional Principles	Collective Principles	Unit Principles		
Game Type Focus	-	SSGs 1v1-4v4 (+GKs) Small Area	LSGs 8v8-10v10 (+GKs) Large Area	MSGs 5v5-7v7 (+GKs) Medium Area	LSGs 8v8-10v10 (+GKs) Small/Med Area	Match Day 11v11
Bout Durations	-	1-3 min	5-10 min	3-5 min	4 min	2 x 45 min
	Mon: Recovery	Tue-Wed: Conditioning		Thu-Fri: Preparation		Perform

* **Training Week based on Professional Microcycle Example** - see pages 20-21.

Key Focus on:

- **Review in Recovery** of the key principles covered across the microcycle (training week)
- Stimulating the **Neural Firing Responses**
- Stimulating **Fast Cognitive Processes**
- Reduced player density ensuring **Minimal Fatigue**

Pre-Match Activation Warm Ups

ACTIVATION TRAINING SESSION
1 Day Until Match (MD +6/-1)

Pre-Match Activation Training Day (45-60 min):

1. Resistance Warm Up (10-12 min)
2. Reaction Speed Conditioning Practice (5-15 min)
3. Large Sided Game in Small/Medium Area (10-50 min)

Pre-Match Activation Warm Ups

1 DAY UNTIL MATCH (MD +6/-1)
Pre-Match Activation Warm Up Practices

INTENSITY: All practices are performed at full intensity

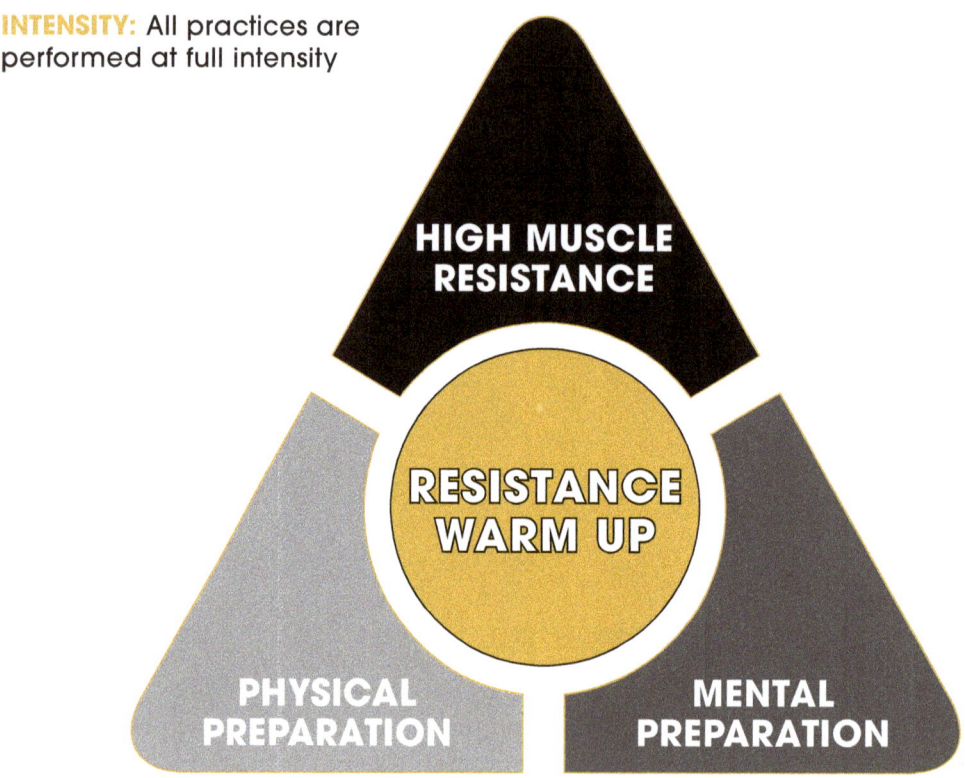

What are Resistance Warm Ups?
- Include many stop and start actions, directional changes, lower level accelerations, and decelerations in tight spaces.
- Activate the muscle groups for the explosive maximum accelerations and decelerations later in the session.
- Provide resistance to the working muscles through explosive actions in small spaces.

Why are they used on this day of the training week (MD +6/-1)?
- To prepare the players for the smaller surface area type work developed through the course of the session.

How does this help to maximise performance?
- Resistance warm ups are used on this day as a way of preparing the players muscles used for changing directions, acceleration and deceleration efforts.
- Resistance warm ups also generally ready the body for the session ahead (small sided games).

Pre-Match Activation Warm Ups

Activation 1. Dynamic Stretching, Movements, and Sprints Double Circle "Juventus Warm Up"

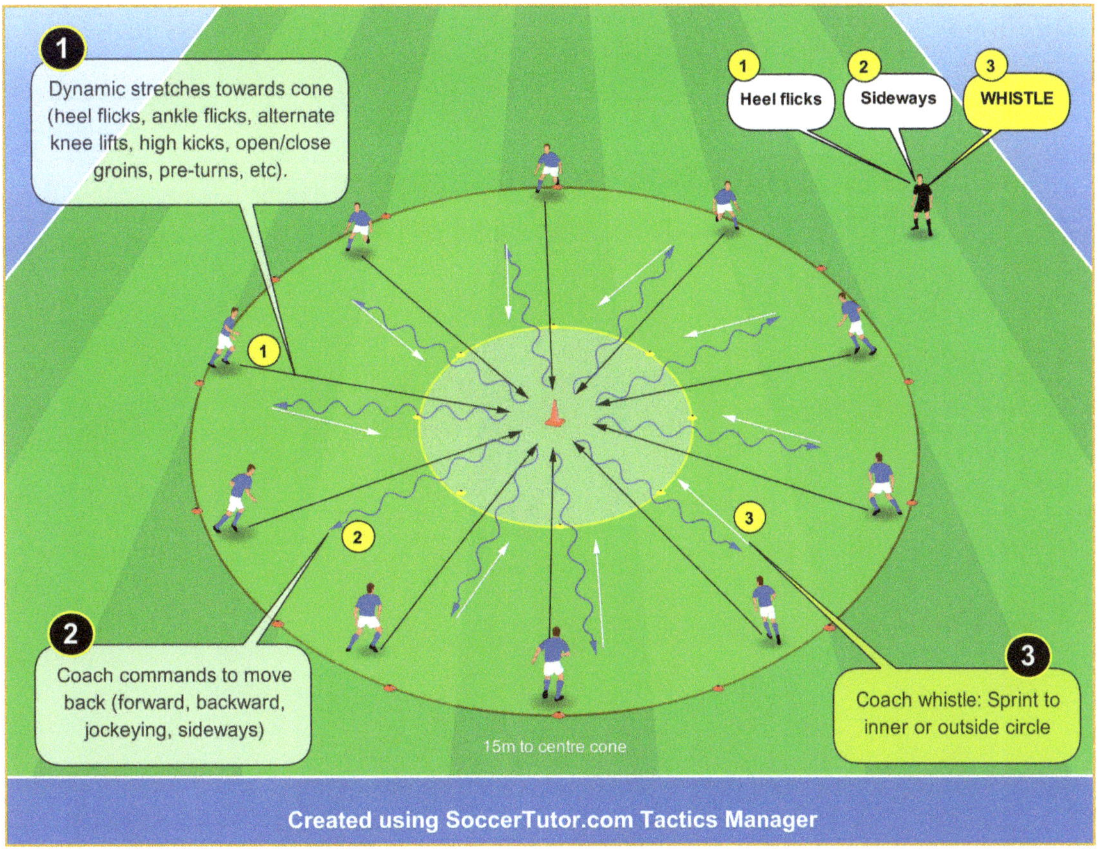

1 Dynamic stretches towards cone (heel flicks, ankle flicks, alternate knee lifts, high kicks, open/close groins, pre-turns, etc).

2 Coach commands to move back (forward, backward, jockeying, sideways)

3 Coach whistle: Sprint to inner or outside circle

1. Heel flicks 2. Sideways 3. WHISTLE

15m to centre cone

Duration	Reps	Sets	Numbers	Size (m)	Work Duration
5-10 min	15 m	15-18	1-20	15 Circle	6-8 min

OBJECTIVE: Dynamic stretching and movements to activate different muscle groups.

- Mark out a large circle and a smaller circle inside it with cones. The players start outside the large circle. The players move from the outside circle performing various dynamic stretches towards the large cone in the centre (heel flicks, ankle flicks, alternate knee lifts, high kicks, open/close groins, pre-turns, etc).

- The coach then commands the players to move back to the outside circle either forward, backwards, jockeying, sideways, (with increasing intensity throughout).

- On the coaches whistle, the players sprint backward, forward, or sideways to the inside or outside of the 2 circles.

Pre-Match Activation Warm Ups

Activation 2. Dynamic Stretching and Different Types of Movements Warm Up

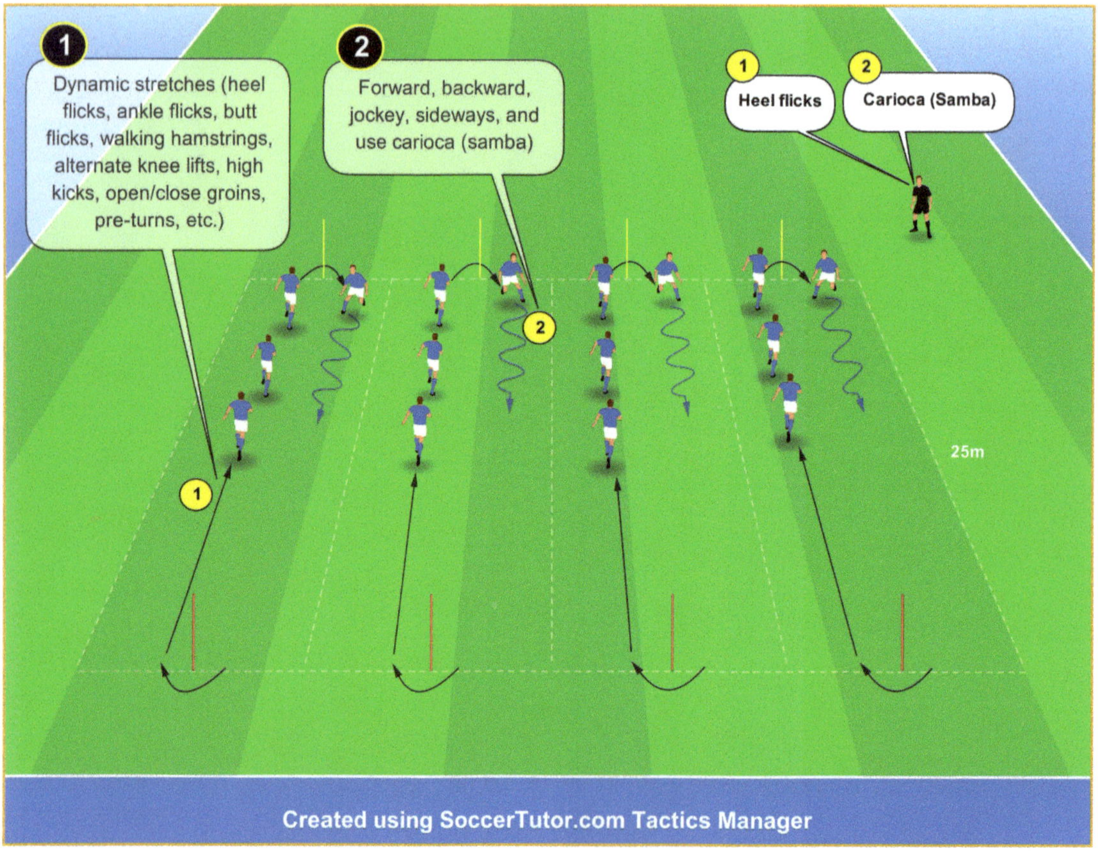

1 Dynamic stretches (heel flicks, ankle flicks, butt flicks, walking hamstrings, alternate knee lifts, high kicks, open/close groins, pre-turns, etc.)

2 Forward, backward, jockey, sideways, and use carioca (samba)

1 Heel flicks **2** Carioca (Samba)

25m

Created using SoccerTutor.com Tactics Manager

Duration	Reps	Sets	Numbers	Size (m)	Work Duration
10-12 min	2 min	3-4	Groups of 4-6	25 Length	6-8 min

OBJECTIVE: Dynamic stretching and movements to activate different muscle groups.

- Players run around the poles and back. The emphasis is on gradually increasing the tempo of the movements. As they do this, the players perform static stretches and dynamic flexibility exercises.

- Include heel flicks, ankle flicks, butt flicks, walking hamstrings, alternate knee lifts, high kicks, open/close groins, pre-turns, etc. Also include various movements so the players go forward, backward, jockey, sideways, and use carioca (samba).

- After 2 minutes, stop and perform some dynamic exercises on the spot.

Pre-Match Activation Warm Ups

Activation 3. Dynamic "Stop & Go" Speed Work with Changes of Direction Warm Up

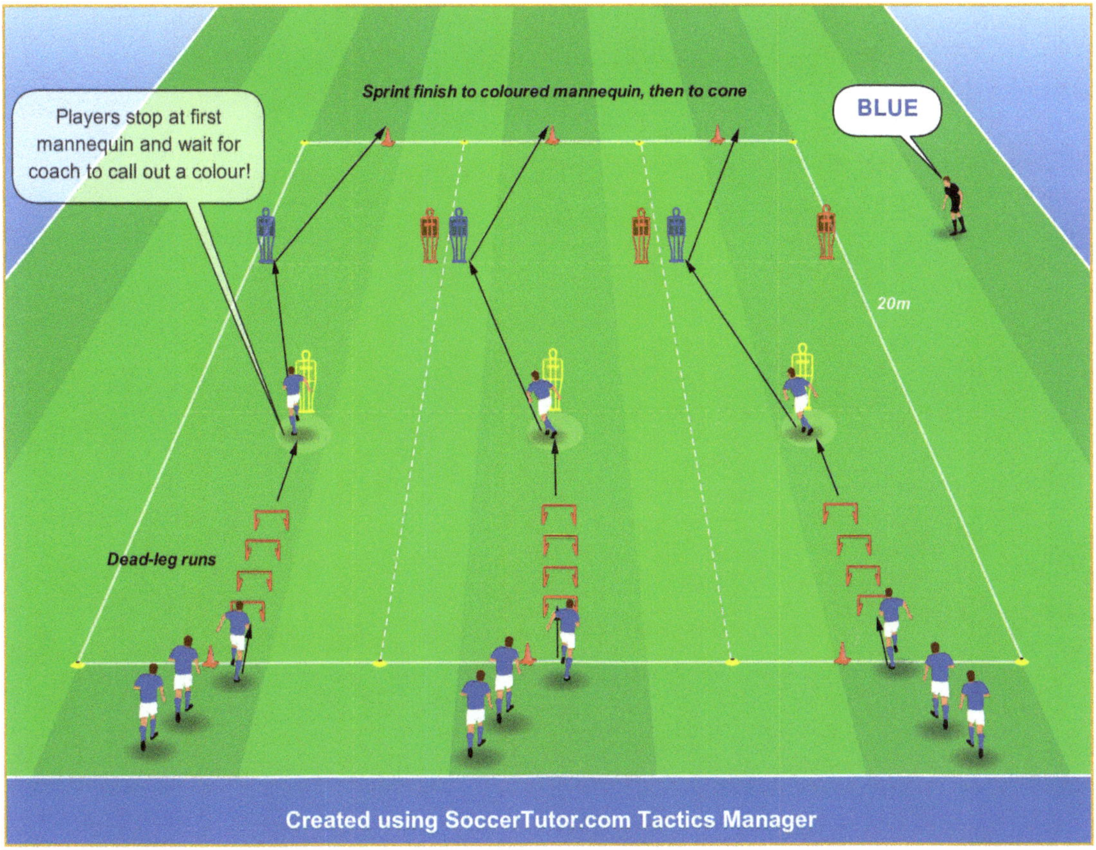

Sprint finish to coloured mannequin, then to cone

BLUE

Players stop at first mannequin and wait for coach to call out a colour!

20m

Dead-leg runs

Created using SoccerTutor.com Tactics Manager

Duration	Reps	Sets	Numbers	Size (m)	Work Duration
5-10 min	4 x 20 m	5	Groups of 4-5	20 Length	6-8 min

OBJECTIVE: Fast feet, agility, coordination, reactions, and neural stimulation.

- We have 3 groups of players in channels, all with 4 hurdles and 1 mannequin in front of them.
- There are also 2 mannequins (or cones) which provide 2 colour options (red and blue), and a cone at the end of the channel.

1. The players perform dead-leg runs through 4 hurdles, move to the mannequin, and are static on their toes.
2. They wait for the coach to call out "**Red**" or "**Blue**" - the players react and sprint to that colour mannequin, then to the cone.
3. The players walk back to the start.

Pre-Match Activation Warm Ups

Activation 4. Dynamic Movement, Agility, Fast Reactions, and Sprinting Warm Up

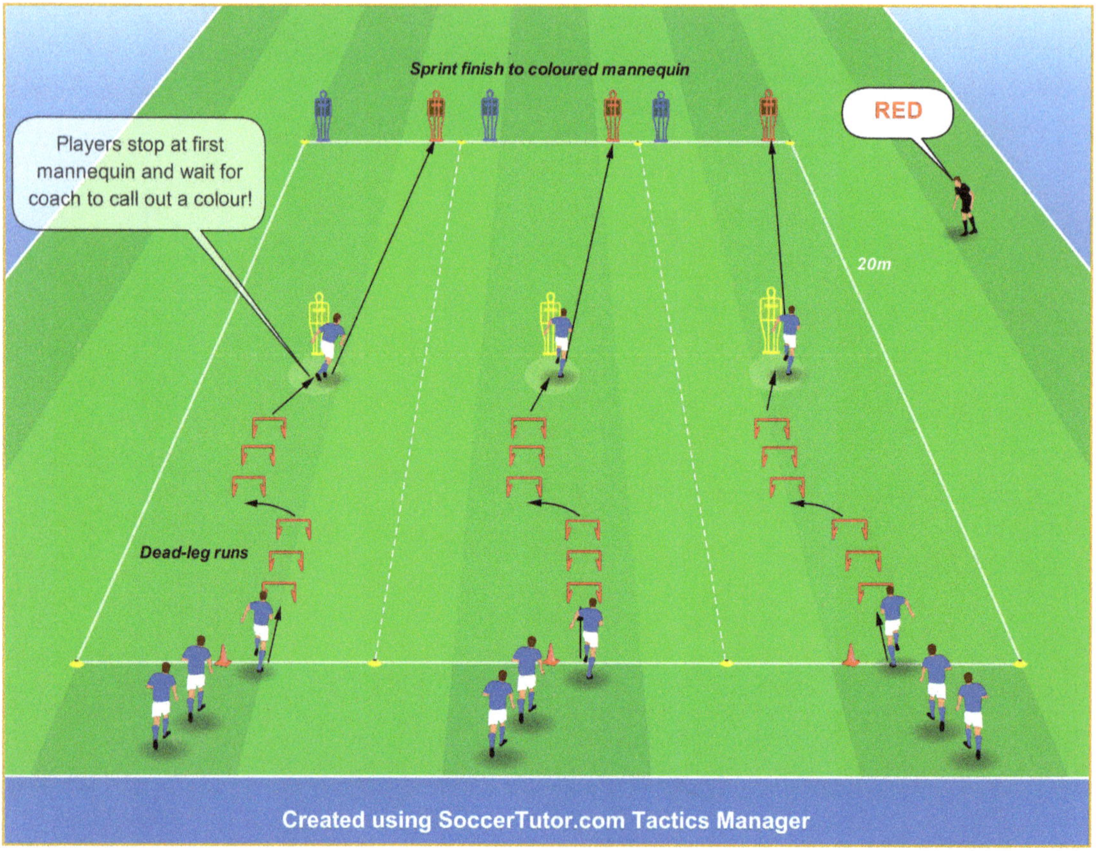

Duration	Reps	Sets	Numbers	Size (m)	Work Duration
5-10 min	4 x 20 m	5	Groups of 4-5	20 Length	6-8 min

OBJECTIVE: Fast feet, agility, coordination, reactions, and neural stimulation.

- We have 3 groups of players in channels, all with 2 sets of 3 hurdles and 1 mannequin in front of them.

- There are also 2 mannequins (or cones) that provide 2 colour options at the end of the channel, which are red and blue in the diagram example.

1. The players perform dead-leg runs through 6 hurdles, move to the mannequin, and are static on their toes.

2. They wait for the coach to call out "**Red**" or "**Blue**" - the players react and sprint to that colour mannequin.

3. The players walk back to the start.

Pre-Match Activation Warm Ups

Activation 5. Mobility Movements and One-Twos in a Dynamic 2 Phase Warm Up Circuit

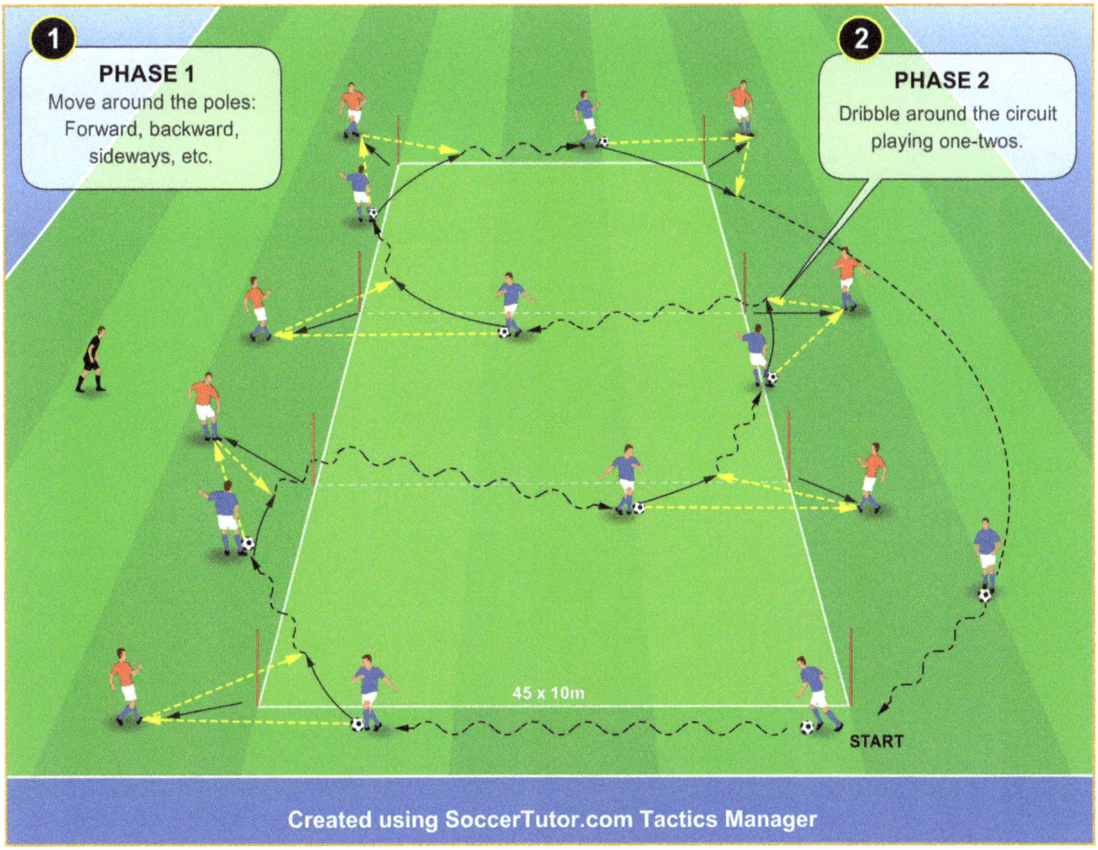

PHASE 1
Move around the poles: Forward, backward, sideways, etc.

PHASE 2
Dribble around the circuit playing one-twos.

45 x 10m

START

Duration	Reps	Sets	Numbers	Size (m)	Work Duration
10 min	30 sec	5	12 +	45 x 10	5 min

OBJECTIVE: Dynamic warm up with passing, receiving, and dribbling.

PHASE 1:

- The players move around the poles (or cones) in single file, one behind the other.
- The different movements are chosen by the coach who leads the group: Forward, backward, sideways, etc.

PHASE 2 (PROGRESSION - DIAGRAM):

- Add 1 player (red) stationed at each pole and give all the other players (blue) a ball.
- As they move around the circuit, the blues play a one-two combination with the red players at the poles, making sure to keep moving forward at all times.

Pre-Match Activation Warm Ups

Activation 6. Quick Combinations and Support Play Passing Square Technical Warm Up

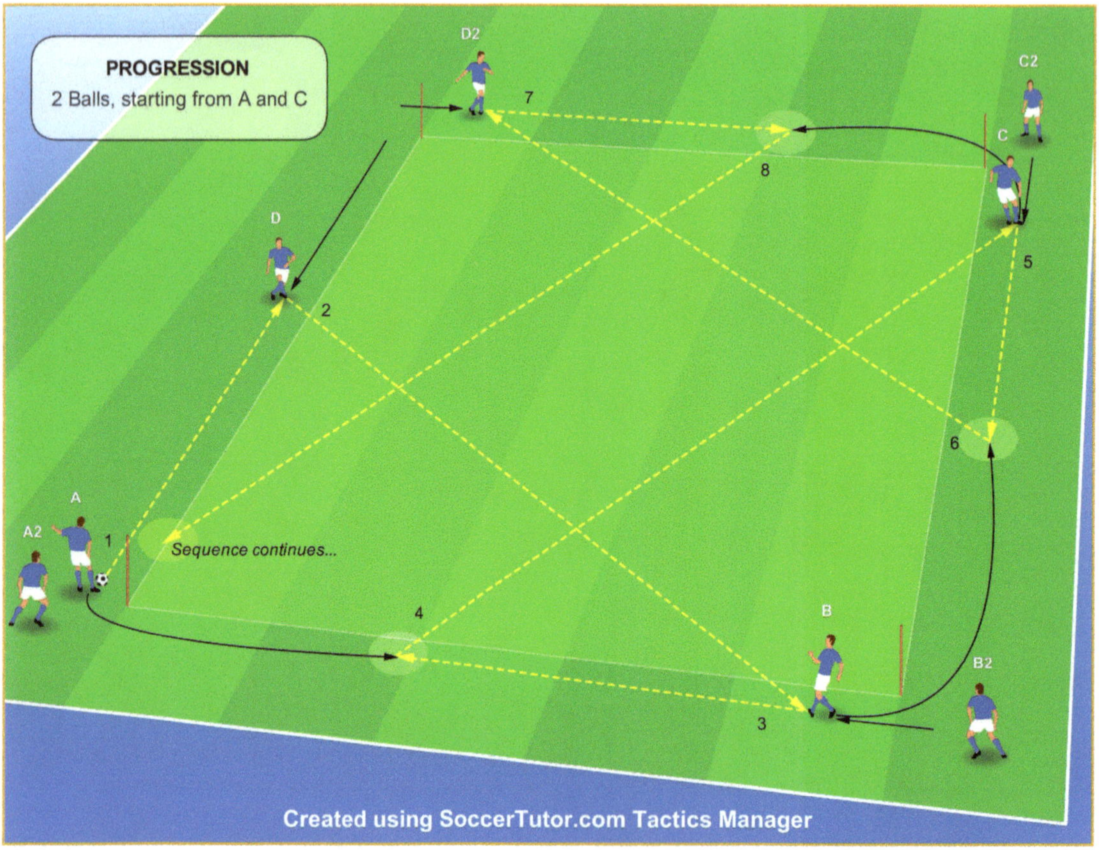

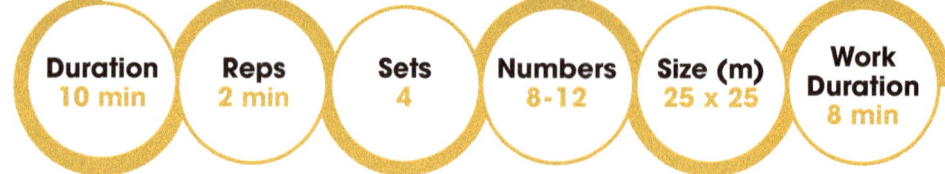

Duration	Reps	Sets	Numbers	Size (m)	Work Duration
10 min	2 min	4	8-12	25 x 25	8 min

OBJECTIVE: Passing, receiving, timing of movement, and combination play.

1. **A** passes to **D**, who drops back.
2. **D** passes diagonally to **B**.
3. **B** sets the ball back for the oncoming **A**.
4. **A** passes diagonally to **C**.
5. **C** sets the ball back for the oncoming **B**.
6. **B** passes diagonally to **D2**.
7. **D2** sets the ball back for the oncoming **C**.
8. **C** passes diagonally to **A** (start) and the same sequence is repeated with **A2**, **B2**, **C2**, and **D2**.

PROGRESSION: Play with 2 balls to increase the intensity of the session.

ADVANCE YOUR CAREER.
BECOME A BETTER COACH...

Accredited & Endorsed Online Football Science & Performance Coaching Courses

The premier global online football education platform, accredited and endorsed by leading universities and elite clubs, which offers cutting-edge courses in football science and performance coaching. Trusted by the football community worldwide, it provides unparalleled expertise and knowledge to aspiring coaches and professionals alike.

www.ISSPF.com / Email: contact@ISSPF.com

    @ISSPFed

ADAM OWEN PERFORMANCE CONSULTANCY

As an esteemed leader and educator in the field of technical and sporting development, performance coaching and football science, AO Performance maintains partnerships with elite football and sports organisations across Europe and beyond. Additionally, collaborations extend to grassroots sports clubs, universities, and FIFA member associations, spanning various levels of expertise. To explore potential collaborations for you or your organisation, reach out to learn more about opportunities now or in the future.

 www.aoperformance.co.uk / Email: contact@aoperformance.co.uk

@adamowen1980

References

- Bangsbo, J., 1994. The physiology of soccer--with special reference to intense intermittent exercise. Acta physiologica scandinavica. Supplementum, 619, pp.1-155.

- Djaoui, L., Chamari, K., Owen, A.L. and Dellal, A., 2017. Maximal sprinting speed of elite soccer players during training and matches. The Journal of Strength & Conditioning Research, 31(6), pp.1509-1517.

- Edholm, P., Krustrup, P. and Randers, M.B., 2015. Half-time re-warm up increases performance capacity in male elite soccer players. Scandinavian journal of medicine & science in sports, 25(1), pp.e40-e49.

- Fashioni, E., Langley, B. and Page, R.M., 2020. The effectiveness of a practical half-time re-warm-up strategy on performance and the physical response to soccer-specific activity. Journal of Sports Sciences, 38(2), pp.140-149.

- Guinoubi, C., Sahli, H., Mekni, R., Abedelmalek, S. and Chamari, K., 2015. Effects of two warm-up modalities on short-term maximal performance in soccer players: didactic modeling. Advances in Physical Education, 5(01), p.70.

- Hills, S.P., Barrett, S., Feltbower, R.G., Barwood, M.J., Radcliffe, J.N., Cooke, C.B., Kilduff, L.P., Cook, C.J. and Russell, M., 2019. A match-day analysis of the movement profiles of substitutes from a professional soccer club before and after pitch-entry. PloS one, 14(1), p.e0211563.

- Malone, S., Owen, A., Mendes, B., Hughes, B., Collins, K. and Gabbett, T.J., 2018. High-speed running and sprinting as an injury risk factor in soccer: can well-developed physical qualities reduce the risk?. Journal of science and medicine in sport, 21(3), pp.257-262.

- Owen, A.L., Dunlop, G., Rouissi, M., Haddad, M., Mendes, B. and Chamari, K., 2016. Analysis of positional training loads (ratings of perceived exertion) during various-sided games in European professional soccer players. International journal of sports science & coaching, 11(3), pp.374-381.

- Owen, A.L., Wong, D.P., Dellal, A., Paul, D.J., Orhant, E. and Collie, S., 2013. Effect of an injury prevention program on muscle injuries in elite professional soccer. The Journal of Strength & Conditioning Research, 27(12), pp.3275-3285.

- Owen, A.L., Wong, D.P., McKenna, M. and Dellal, A., 2011. Heart rate responses and technical comparison between small-vs. large-sided games in elite professional soccer. The journal of strength & conditioning research, 25(8), pp.2104-2110.

- Romaratezabala, E., Nakamura, F.Y., Castillo, D., Gorostegi-Anduaga, I. and Yanci, J., 2018. Influence of warm-up duration on physical performance and psychological perceptions in handball players. Research in Sports Medicine, 26(2), pp.230-243.

- Taylor, K.L., Sheppard, J.M., Lee, H. and Plummer, N., 2009. Negative effect of static stretching restored when combined with a sport specific warm-up component. Journal of Science and Medicine in Sport, 12(6), pp.657-661.

- Walker, O., 2024. Explanation of Warm-Ups. https://www.scienceforsport.com/warm-ups/

- Yanci, J., Iturri, J., Castillo, D., Pardeiro, M. and Nakamura, F.Y., 2019. Influence of warm-up duration on perceived exertion and subsequent physical performance of soccer players. Biology of Sport, 36(2), pp.125-131.

- Zois, J., Bishop, D.J., Ball, K. and Aughey, R.J., 2011. High-intensity warm-ups elicit superior performance to a current soccer warm-up routine. Journal of science and medicine in sport, 14(6), pp.522-528.

Free Trial

Football Coaching Specialists Since 2001

Tactics Manager

Create your own Practices, Tactics & Plan Sessions!

Tactics Manager App

SoccerTutor.com

Football Coaching Specialists Since 2001

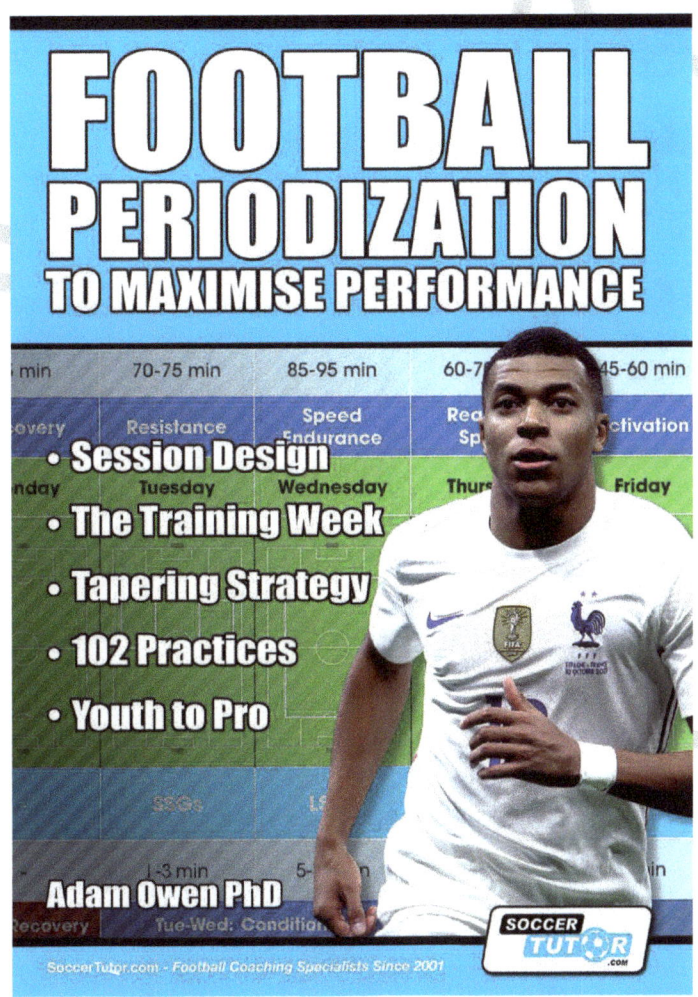

Coaching Books Available in Full Colour Print and eBook!
PC | Mac | iPhone | iPad | Android Phone / Tablet | Chromebook

 **FREE** Coach Viewer **APP**

SoccerTutor.com

Football Coaching Specialists Since 2001

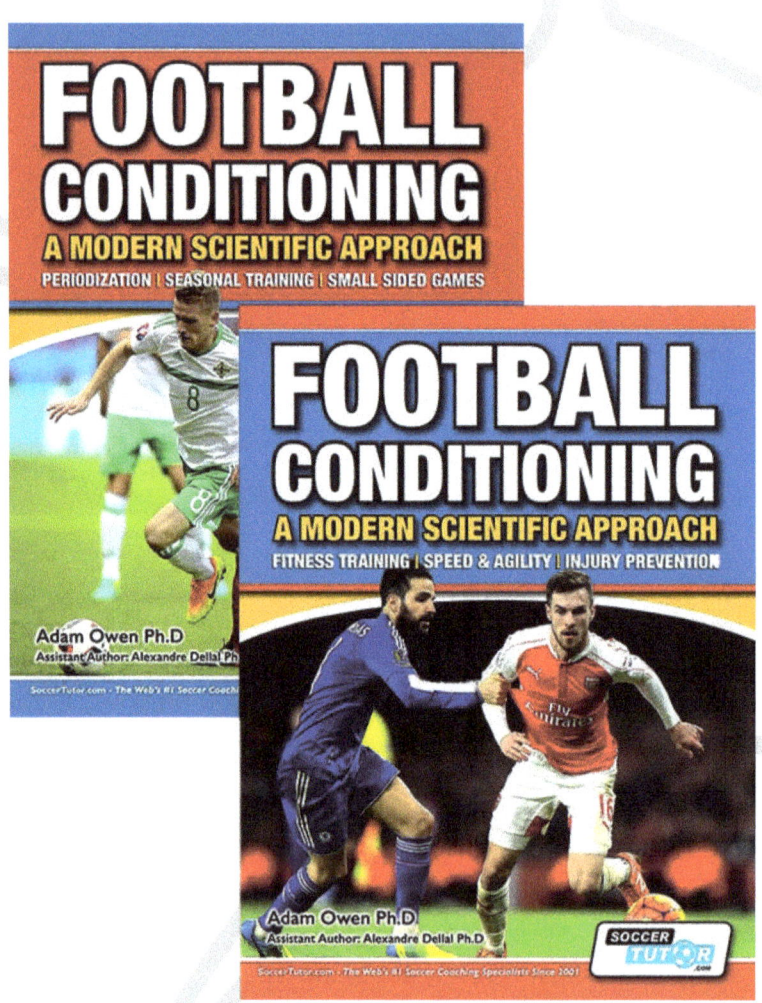

Coaching Books Available in Full Colour Print and eBook!
PC | Mac | iPhone | iPad | Android Phone / Tablet | Chromebook

 **FREE** Coach Viewer **APP**

SoccerTutor.com

Coming Soon!

Football Coaching Specialists Since 2001

TECHNICAL
To Maximise Performance

- 50 Practices
- Youth to Pro
- Training Week
- Football Periodization

Available in Full Colour Print and eBook!

www.ingramcontent.com/pod-product-compliance
Lightning Source LLC
Chambersburg PA
CBHW061210230426
43665CB00028B/2967